D1416856

Talking, Thinking, Growing

Talking, Thinking, Growing

Language with the Young Child

JOAN TOUGH

SCHOCKEN BOOKS · NEW YORK

First SCHOCKEN edition 1974

98760

10127/77 Ret 7.50

Contents

Introduction to the American Edition

IN writing this book my intention has been to consider the development and use of language by young children in a practical and nontheoretical way, drawing illustrations from recorded examples of talk between children, between mothers and children, and between teachers and children. By relying on examples to make my points, I have, without doubt, tended to present an oversimplified view of the process of interaction in the family, particularly as it proceeds between mother and child. The variety and complexity of the combination of forces that produce the home environment and provide the child with continuous linguistic experiences should not be underestimated.

Primarily I have been concerned to demonstrate the extent to which the child is dependent upon communication with adults for building up the widest possible range of resources of language and of strategies for learning which the use of language makes possible. The child's capacity for thinking clearly cannot match the adult's; but it is only because adults express their sophisticated thinking in their talk—in situations in which the child can search for clues to their meanings—that he can attempt to meet and share such ways of thinking.

What I have written in the following pages might be judged to have been arrived at through patient observation of children talking with each other, of mothers talking with their young children, and of teachers talking in their nursery and infant schools. Observation has played a major part in my study, but observation also reveals that there is no agreed view of what constitutes the best way of talking with, or for that matter, of bringing up, children. There is no agreement, either, about the best ways of helping those children who are at a disadvantage in education because of their apparent inability to use language for effective communication in school. Indeed, some may even feel that our efforts should be directed toward different goals.

It is, therefore, reasonable for those who read this book to ask by what evidence I am persuaded to take up the position and advocate methods of talking with children that I have indicated here. Books which are now being prepared (Tough, in preparation, and Tough and Sestini, in preparation)—an account of a longitudinal study of children's development of uses of language between the ages of three and seven-and-a-half years, and a study of the way in which their mothers communicate—will give more substantial support to the views expressed here. Meanwhile, for those who may be interested, I indicate briefly the sources of theory and research that have influenced my thinking.

Several assumptions underlie my arguments. The first and quite central issue is that the development of language makes an important contribution to the course of the child's cognitive development. The work of Vygotsky, carried out in the U.S.S.R. some forty years ago but not made available in English until much more recently (Vygotsky, 1962), is impressive. Words help the child to develop concepts, because each time a particular word is used the child's attention is drawn to one more instance of the concept. Vygotsky's view is that, in time, words come to represent generalized notions abstracted from many experiences. Hearing words, according to Vygotsky, assists the child to order and classify his experiences; using words offers him a means of testing hypotheses about their meanings. Moreover, the motivation to respond to and use language stems from the need to communicate, particularly from the need to communicate with adults. Vygotsky holds that the development of concepts, other than those that can be abstracted directly from concrete experience, must be dependent on the language of the tutoring adult, at least until the extension of ideas can be reached through reading.

If we accept Vygotsky's view, then language is seen to play a critical part in conceptual development. On the other hand, Piaget and his colleagues in Geneva, and many who have replicated their work, stress that the child's thought stems from his own actions, that is, from the information supplied by his sensori-motor activity. It is the child's own actions that establish inner frames of reference which are the basis of meaning. Language is important because it "may increase the powers of thought in range and rapidity" (Piaget and Inhelder, 1969, p. 86), because language allows quick reference to a sequence of actions or to a structure built from numerous actions. In Piaget's view, language frees the child's thinking from the restrictions of the ongoing present situation. But what the child can do with language, the kind of thinking he can express through language, is seen to be dependent on the developmental level of his inner nonverbal frames of reference.

Although the views of Piaget and Vygotsky are often presented as being in opposition, this does not seem to be the only possible conclusion. They can also be seen as complementary and equally valid views of the part played by language in cognitive development. The language of others plays a part in stimulating, and setting value on, the child's actions: the child's actions, his responses to his experiences, provide an essential basis for meaning: the presence of language as part of his experiences motivates the child to seek for meaning in what he hears. Both views are needed to explain how language and thinking each support and provoke the other.

A second assumption underlying the views expressed in this book is that there are important differences in the experiences children have of language in use. Although children tend to have similar concrete experiences from which meanings for basic concepts are drawn, some important differences in their experiences stem from differences in the way in which parents view their children and from differences in the way of life of families. Not only will values and relationships be different, but these will affect both the content of the language used and the form in which it is used.

This assumption reflects the hypothesis put forward by Whorf (1958) that the way in which the individual perceives and responds to the world around him is largely determined by the language forms and speech patterns that surround him and which he can hardly escape learning to use. These language forms and speech patterns carry with them values and attitudes, and direct the child's attention to aspects of experience that the users see as significant or that they have assimilated and take for granted.

The Whorfian view has led to research that examines differences between the practices in families from different sections of the population, between which it can be anticipated that there will be differences in both attitudes and traditions. Bernstein's work is prominent in this field: through a program of research his now well-known theory has developed (Bernstein, 1971; Bernstein, ed., 1973). He and his colleagues have shown that there are significant differences between the language used by children from sections of the population differentiated by experiences of work and of education, that is, by social class.

In America the investigation has a wider basis since differences in the population stem not only from the class structure but also from the multi-cultural nature of the population. A great deal of research has established that there are differences in the language used by children that are strongly associated with the social status of the parents. Among others are studies by Deutsch (1965), Loban (1963), and Strickland (1962). Since such differences have been clearly shown to exist, inevitably research has focused also on the means by which such differences come about. Language is learned in the years before school, so attention has naturally centered on the interaction between mother and child, which seems likely to provide the main experiences from which the child will learn to use language.

In Britain there has been, so far, little direct study of talk between mother and child. However, a longitudinal study of children between the ages of three and seven-and-a-half years has shown that between-class differences are already well established by the age of three and continue to develop (Tough, in preparation). There have been several studies of mothers' responses to questions that ask them to say what they would do or say in hypothetical situations. In several studies (Brandis and Henderson, 1970; Bernstein and Henderson, 1969; and Robinson and Rackstraw, 1967), significant differences have been found between working-class and middle-class mothers in the view they take of their children, the purposes for which they report talking with their children, and how they would answer their children's questions.

Studies that rely on interview techniques make the assumption that reported practice is likely to give a genuine picture of actual practice and it is difficult to judge to what extent this assumption is justified. However, the way in which mothers organize answers to questions in an interview is likely to indicate the kind of experiences of language in use that they will provide for their children at some time. As part of the longitudinal study referred to above, Elizabeth Sestini has made a study of the way in which mothers answered questions about their children, school, and education (Tough and Sestini, in preparation). This work provides considerable support for the view that there are likely to be between-class differences in the meanings that are being made available to children as their mothers talk with them.

Recording mothers talking with their children has been undertaken in several studies in the United States. Roger Brown and his associates were early in the field as they attempted to discover the sequence in which the child acquired speech. This work centered on the way in which the child learned to order those elements of speech he could produce and related this to what he was hearing in his mother's talk (Brown and Bellugi, eds., 1964). More recently Baldwin and Frank (1967) have studied the way in which mothers talk with their young children and have found that generally mothers reduce the grammatical complexity of their language when addressing their three-year-old children. Phillips (1970) and Snow (1971), studying the interaction of mother and child in different contexts, offer supporting evidence for this. Brown and his colleagues, however, have also produced evidence which indicates that when responding to the child's talk the parents focus their attention on the meaning of what the child says rather than on grammatical errors (Brown, Cazden, and Bellugi, 1969).

Robert Hess and his colleague, however, were the first to test the Whorfian hypothesis as it had been reformulated by Bernstein. The comparison of upper- and lower-class mothers talking with their children as they instructed them in learning a simple skill revealed differences in what were described as "teaching styles." Hess and Shipman (1965) concluded that the children of lower-class mothers were not only being offered different meanings for their experiences, but that this actually resulted in a deprivation of meaning, in that meaning that was an intrinsic part of the situation was not made clear to the child. These same children were followed from pre-school into the primary grades and it was then found that maternal teaching styles related to the children's school performance (Hess *et al.*, 1967).

Once it had been established that there were differences in children's use of language that were associated with social status, attention turned to an examination of methods of improving or accelerating the development of language skills by lower-class children. However, a good deal of controversy has arisen in the United States, and is perhaps reflected in Britain, because of implicit values that underlie much of the research into children's language. The problem of finding ways of analyzing speech data has meant that a number of linguistic indices have had to be relied upon—for example, mean length of utterances, complexity in the structure of the utterances, complexity or elaboration in the noun and verb phrases. Labov (1970) has been foremost in challenging the inference which has followed from using such methods, that some children need instruction in the use of linguistic structures. Labov has himself shown that in informal conversation among themselves the language of lower-class black youths is as well formed and complete in structure as that of their upper-class peers. There is perhaps no real conflict between the Labov and the Bernstein position: there may be no differences between the groups in their ability to communicate with their peers, but there may be differences in other contexts. It is the content of what is to be communicated that is important—that is, the meaning that is being made explicit, the ideas that are being expressed. Peer-group talk is important for the social well-being of individuals but it may not facilitate their success in education. The evidence seems to be that many children may be at a disadvantage in school because of their lack of facility in the communication of certain kinds of meaning. For their communication skills to be improved, it would seem that new facility in using language for purposes which are important but unfamiliar should be sought.

It is to this end that programs for the pre-school child have been developed. In the United States many experimental programs have been conducted with groups of pre-school children, and many have shown that children have made gains, both in the use of language and in general attainment, as a result. Whether such gains can be maintained through the first years of school has not yet been shown. In a recent paper Bartlett has analyzed twenty-one such programs (Cazden, ed., 1972). Only one of these, Talk Reform (Gahagan and Gahagan, 1970), originated in Britain as part of the work of Bernstein's team. Although these programs have different emphases, there is also much in common between most of them. Importance is attached to activities that encourage cognitive and social awareness and the development of concepts, particularly basic mathematical and locational concepts; there is stress on the augmentation of general vocabulary and of teaching syntax. Some programs concentrate on problem-solving activities and the development of logical reasoning. In her paper Bartlett makes a comparison among the contents of the twenty-one programs she surveyed.

However, the introduction of structured programs as part of the Head Start policy has aroused considerable controversy, because of the inferences on which such programs are based. In 1971 Robert Hess and his associates outlined four basic models that were being put forward to account for the differences in educational and intellectual attainment between sub-groups and the dominant group in the United

States population. In Britain the same trends are reflected in the present discussion of what the aims of pre-school education should be and what form pre-school education should take.

If the disadvantaged child is regarded as coming from a home that has denied learning to its children, the child is viewed as *deficient* in some way. This was the view from which Head Start was conceived, and the aim was to make good the accumulated deficit by the time the child came into school. Thus programs like that by Gray and Klaus (1965), Deutsch (1962), and the early phases of the Ypsilanti Pre-School Project, according to its director (Silverman and Weikart), were openly programs of intervention out to reform the pre-school child, teaching him particular cognitive skills it was assumed he had been deprived of by his home.

If, however, the explanation for the between-class differences in attainment in school is seen to be the rejection of lower-class children by schools that rob them of confidence and teach them that failure is inevitable, then the focus for change is centered on the school and on teachers. Programs are designed to supply the teacher with the required skills; learning is to be enjoyed; success for the child must be assured, his confidence in himself boosted by praise and reward. Perhaps the Peabody Language Development Kit is an example of programs designed on this basis.

A third way of explaining the differences in attainment between children from upper and lower social groups, or from sub-culture and the dominant culture, is to assert that people are different, and that sub-groups have different strengths and values. Such differences, it is claimed, have not been appreciated by schools. Failure for many children then is seen to be the result of a failure in communication between teachers and children and parents and school, and a failure to build on the strengths of individuals. Strengths are to be valued and variety is to be seen as a source of richness for all. Thus a policy that accepts the pluralistic nature of society, valuing all skills equally, is to be promoted. The conflict of maintaining such a view in education, when clearly educational attainment is valued and rewarded by the society it serves, can be imagined.

A fourth view has also been expressed, both in the United States and in Britain. This view sees the lower-class child, like his parents, as the victim of the social structure. Solutions are to be found only in changing that structure. In this view, schools are not so much irrelevant but form an important agency for maintaining the status quo. Only by placing power in the hands of parents and pupils will it be possible to change the way in which schools function.

These four views are different perspectives of the same problem. Seen from different standpoints, the solutions offered are different. But what of the teacher? How shall the teacher conceptualize the problem? What role can the teacher play in meeting the problem?

The theme of this book is that many children are at a disadvantage in school because the meaning that underlies certain crucial modes of thinking and using language have not been made relevant and accessible to them. Both teacher and child contribute to the problem. The child unwittingly finds himself in an environment in which skills with which he is unfamiliar are relied on heavily for the transmission of the content of his education. He still awaits experiences that would promote the development of these skills, although it may be that his early learning and practiced use of language provide some hindrance to their easy accomplishment. The teacher contributes to the problem if she fails to diagnose the cause and fails to provide experiences from which he would benefit most.

There are those who would see the responsibility for the child's continued failure resting entirely with the teacher. But it must be remembered that until relatively recently silence was the rule for children in school: value has not been set on talk in the past. Reading and writing have been the accepted methods of communication in school, with the teacher's talk fulfilling the purposes of instruction. The role of language, and particularly the part played by the dialogue between adult and child in general cognitive development, has been recognized by few, and it is only in the last decade that the language development of children has been a major focus for research.

There is now new information to guide the teacher's practice, and new insight into the importance of language should bring about changes in attitudes and new understanding of the problem. The teacher's attention can now turn to the means by which the child's disadvantage might be overcome.

But there are also those who see the problems of the disadvantaged child being solved only by bringing about radical changes in the behavior of parents who, left to themselves, fail to establish in their young children skills that are needed in school. In Britain this is a view often expressed in the current debate about the form that early childhood education should take and the part that parents should play. But to rely on developing skills, which some parents have acquired as a result of their upbringing or extended education (and probably both), in parents who gained little from their years in school may be to underestimate the complexity of changing established attitudes, values, and accepted and well-practiced modes of thinking and talking. The result may be to deflect attention from the child's problems and make parents feel, as they never have before, responsible for the child's failure, with little benefit to the child. Could success be guaranteed even if parents tried to follow the instructions of their new teachers?

Without a doubt there is often a lack of communication between teachers and parents, particularly between teachers and parents of disadvantaged children. A major task for schools must be to overcome this failure in communication and to find ways of gaining the interest of all parents.

But the dangers of a policy that chooses to help children indirectly through educating their parents, or to rely on parents as the teaching force, is likely only to increase the disadvantage of the already disadvantaged child. If such opinion prevails, it may be that the opportunities will be missed for giving the child early, regular, and continued contact with a teacher who knows how to extend his thinking and his use of language, and who encourages the interest and participation of parents because of the support these give to the child's learning.

The teacher's main responsibility must be for the young children in her care. How can she promote the cognitive and social development of all? This is the crux of the problem. How many young children can one teacher cater for? How can schools be changed so that a full cognitive and social development is possible for all? High among the teacher's priorities must come the need to develop communication skills. High among the priorities of those who shape educational policy ought to come the provision of well-qualified teachers in sufficient numbers to make sure that during the early years in school an environment is created in which all children will succeed in establishing skills vital to their later education and to their lives as educated citizens.

Talking, Thinking, Growing

Chapter 1

The Beginning of the
Child's Language

Two little girls stand in the corner of the nursery, apparently oblivious of the activity of the other children around them. Both are three years old. Alison picks up the edges of her skirt and pirouettes, trying to balance on one foot. She stops, a little out of breath, and calls to Jill:

Alison: Watch me, Jill—watch what I can do.

Again she twists, lifting her foot and bending her knee. Jill is spurred to action: she jumps up and down, up and down.

Jill: I can skip—I can—watch me.
Alison: I've got a skipping rope at home and I can skip properly.
Jill: I can—I can, too.
Alison: I can jump high. Look!

Alison jumps up and down.

Jill: Watch me, Alison—Alison.

Jill now stands quite still as though thinking hard.

Jill: You know—I know another Alison—and she's my friend—and she lives—she lives just now—across—just opposite me. She lives at 2 Oak Villas. She doesn't go to school now—she's not very old—just now she's not—but wait till she gets bigger—till she's four or eight—and then she'll go to school.
Alison: To nursery school you mean, of course.
Jill: Yes, and then she'll go—you see she'll go—she'll go to school—and she'll be a new person to go to school.

Jill ends on a triumphant note.

Jill: You see—that's it—a new person to go to school.

As Jill finishes speaking she jumps up and down, apparently
with delight at what she has just said.

This sample, from a recording of Jill's conversations during one
morning in the nursery really needs to be heard for her effort to
be fully appreciated. It is as though she were wrestling to capture
some of the meaning which for her adhered to the name Alison
and to transform it into a few words in order that this other
Alison should share her knowledge. With each expression of an
idea there is a quickening of the movement of her face and body.
Jill tilts her head to look at Alison, smiles, eyes glinting, as she
hurries to produce through words a bit more of her own inner
world for her playmate to share. Her voice lifts to a peak of
intonation, and then she refocuses and the attention she has
given to Alison wanes, and her voice fades away.
    She pauses, her eyes lose their lustre. They brighten again and
she embarks on a further stretch of speech, gathering speed
until a new climax is reached and then her voice fades to a
whisper again. Within lies the image, the knowledge of her
friend—the meaning which is attached for her to the name
Alison. Within, too, is a store of knowledge of language from
which she selects and transposes into the utterances which we
hear. We cannot see the working of the child's mind; we can
only infer from the behaviour we observe that Jill searches for
a form of language which will hold and display her particular
meaning to this other Alison whose presence and name sparked
off her flow of ideas.
    We can see that Jill's memory allows her to consider her
friend, although this Alison is, at the time, miles away from her.
The exact position of Alison's house in the street is recalled.
There is considerable effort to retrieve the word 'opposite'
following her first attempt 'across', so she refines her meaning.
She stops and thinks again: 'she doesn't go to school.' Once
more her voice fades, she stands very still, her eyes once more
withdraw attention from Alison. The pause lengthens—and then
another spurt 'wait until she's bigger—and then—and then.'

Again she is very still, again the pause extends, her whole body tenses and at last her eyes brighten, her face lights up and she returns her attention to Alison, bending to look into her face as she cries:

She'll be a *new person* to go to school.

The impression is that this is a completely original idea, wrung from within, created by Jill, as though emerging for the first time and recognised with a flash of new understanding. Jill's talk has served not only to communicate her ideas to her playmate but the very activity seems to have created new meaning for her.

As we consider Jill's performance here we might be struck by the complexity of the mechanisms of the brain which makes this behaviour possible. Yet, perhaps if we had heard this same piece of conversation in the nursery, it would have passed by, its emergence scarcely noted. Spoken words have so short an existence that they are gone before they can be fully examined.

The short response of Jill's playmate is also quite remarkable. This seven-word utterance would perhaps have passed completely without notice in the normal way. Through Jill's long and hesitant speech, Alison shows that she follows and understands. She nods from time to time, and then shows how closely she has followed Jill's ideas by her short, dry seven-word utterance, which conveys with it a slight air of superiority:

To nursery school you mean, of course!

Alison has not only followed, but has been checking what she hears with the meaning the words have for her, and she finds them inadequate. She deduces that the reference is to 'nursery school' and not to the other 'school' she knows, which her sister attends. 'School' and 'nursery school' have different meanings, and she modifies the received information to match her own meaning.

The reader may say that we have inferred a great deal about the mental activity which lies behind Jill's and Alison's observable behaviour. This is true, but it is clear that something does take place: it is as though each child has his own private model of the world built from the experiences he has had of it. This private world of his consists not only of places and people and things, and of relationships between them, but of the feelings through which he relates to the external world. These images, impressions and feelings, within each individual child, provide the source of his own particular set of meanings.

As this recording shows, Jill and Alison already have considerable skill in using language to organise their own meanings in order to communicate with others. Yet less than three years before, as tiny babies, meaning for them was of a very rudimentary kind. How is it possible to move from the state of the baby, for whom meaning can be no more than the contrast between comfort and discomfort, and the sounds they voice no more than symptoms of these two conditions, to this very complex behaviour which implies the existence of a well developed system of meanings?

In the first place, the child's mother responds to the child's crying because of the meaning it has for her—she hurries to comfort him, to attend to his needs. In time, therefore, the child comes to associate his own crying with the attention and the ending of discomfort which it brings. At an early age the child seems to hush his cries as footsteps or familiar voices are heard, and by the end of the second or third month he has learnt to differentiate some of his experiences. He learns, for example, to expect the way in which his mother handles and fondles him, and protests when he is handled by some other person in a different way. Meaning for him is in that with which he becomes familiar because of its regular occurrence. Gradually, meaning is extended to the recognition of faces, and perhaps voices, as a part differentiated, and reacted to differently, from the rest of his experiences.

During the third and fourth months, the baby's impetus to gain strength and achieve control of his own movements helps him to differentiate the various qualities of his immediate environment. Distinctions such as those between hard and soft, warm and cold, resistant and non-resistant, restricted and unrestricted, must begin to emerge. This meaning is held for him in his muscles, in the soles of the feet, in the fingers and palm of the hands, in the mouth and the tongue. Meaning is derived from repeated similar experiences which build up expectations about what will follow.

An outcome of this period, in which pleasure comes from greater control and movement, is the growth of intention to move, to touch, to feel and to taste whatever he comes into contact with. This activity brings its own extension of meaning for the child. A second outcome arises from the greater control of the tongue, the throat and the mouth. Sounds emerge as a result of this exploratory activity, to which people respond as though the baby had spoken, and they smile and talk to him. This encounter obviously gives pleasure to both the baby and the adult. In the first place the adult reacts to the baby's gurgling, but a little later the baby will respond to the adult's approach with a distinct concentration and effort. Sometimes the sound fails to come and we see the baby making all the movements, chucking his chin and pursing his lips, perhaps with nothing emerging but a breathy sound and a bubble. Here is the pre-runner of speech—the intention to make sound; the imitation is crude, it is true, that of repaying vocalisation with vocalisation, and not of reproducing the identical sound itself, but nevertheless, it forms the basis for an exchange which carries some of the qualities of conversation, and for the development of social meaning.

The child moves even nearer to the act of communication when he takes the step of initiating such a 'conversation,' intentionally attracting the attention of the adult by babbling, or letting out a squeal, and clearly waiting for the adult's response. And with each new development comes a new awareness and recognition of some aspect of his experience; the baby responds to the world on the basis of the meanings it has for him. His bottle now means for him food. His coat and bonnet may mean the pram outside and the familiar street; the bark of a dog may lead him to seek to look for the family pet. From about the fifth or sixth month onwards the presence of language around him will more and more aid him to distinguish people, objects and events and help him to extract new meaning from his experience.

Since we all expect the child to begin to talk we intuitively help him to attach some kind of meaning to particular sounds which he produces. During the babbling stage we can see that sounds like 'mama' or 'mum-mum,' 'mammam' or 'mom-mom' are part of every baby's vocal repertoire. He tends to make this kind of articulation by pressing his lips together as he anticipates the satisfaction of his hunger. He frets a little, making the movements with his lips which are the movements he makes when feeding—almost as though he tries to reproduce the feeding by enacting his own part in it. Mothers the world over, as they respond to the child's hunger fretting, attach this sound to themselves saying the equivalent of 'Ma-ma's coming, don't cry now!' Since mother responds frequently to the child's murmurings of 'ma-ma,' and indeed delightedly responds as though the child has called for her, gradually the child attaches the meaningfulness of her presence to this sound. Later he will call 'ma-ma' in a deliberate attempt to bring mother as a person to him to restore his well-being, his comfort, his security, and to bring the satisfaction of hearing the familiar voice, and seeing the familiar face.

It is because mother and the family view his prowess and achievement with great pleasure, using speech in the attempt to convey this pleasure, that the child is urged into speech. The important thing is that we do respond as though we expect the child to talk. We recognise particular sounds within his repertoire which are repeated again and again. Perhaps all babies produce the sounds, da-da, gee-gee, bye-bye, ba-ba, coo-coo, ted-ted, ta-ta and others. At this stage he appears to have some control over the production of these sounds—that is, he can produce them on demand and by deliberate imitation. The family works hard to attach their own meanings to them. Thus they wave to him and say 'bye-bye' as they leave him. Someone may take his hand and wave it and say 'bye-bye' and this is done so often that eventually the child repeats the gesture and the sound in response to the person who is going away. The child may then, at some point, demonstrate his understanding of the meaning of this routine when, unprompted, he performs the same ritual as he is taken out of the house, or he may even issue it as a directive to someone, indicating that he wants them to leave.

During this period between nine or ten months of age and

eighteen months or so, other people intuitively help the child to attach meaning to much of his 'natural' vocal repertoire. Here is the origin of so-called 'baby' talk which may include 'baby' names for brothers and sisters, for the family pets, for some familiar objects and for some clear demands for action, such as 'more-more,' 'gen-gen' (again-again), and 'down now.'

Parents often worry about this baby language, and wonder whether they should encourage the child to adopt terms like 'gee-gee' or whether they should wait until the child is older and able to control articulation and produce the sound 'horse.' Some mothers insist that the child should quite definitely not be encouraged to develop such baby talk. The 'baby talk' period, however, would seem to be important because, common sense suggests, by attaching meaning to sounds the child demonstrates that he can make, he may be offered clues to what language is about. Because he has 'words' which obviously bring attention to his wants when he issues them, he may more readily strive for others when he has recognised the references which are being made.

It is clear also, that the child is often able to respond to words appropriately before he is able to produce them himself. This is because the whole situation provides a clear demonstration of meaning. 'Catch the ball' may apparently be understood in a situation where the thrower is tossing the ball to the child, and although responding appropriately to this phrase, the child may not be able to produce any of it. Meaning for the child lies, perhaps, in the direction of movement, the impetus of the body, the sight and feel of the ball and of the pleasurable relationship which exists between himself and his companion who plays ball with him.

We are often surprised by the toddler who behaves intelligently in what appears to be an entirely verbal situation. For example, 'Where did I put my slippers?' father says looking round the kitchen, and the eighteen-month-old child may be seen to hurry upstairs and to return with the slippers, obviously waiting for acclamation at his cleverness. But this is a familiar situation for the child, which is enacted each day. A key part of the father's utterance may be the word 'slippers' which triggers off reference to the child's own meaning: meaning for him is in the memory of father's blue slippers lying in the bedroom. The child learns to use 'clues' to the situation, of which the utterance is only a part. He has now built up a great deal of 'meaning' from everyday living: the speech used by people around him and to him is an important part of that experience.

This may sound as though we are belittling the child's achievement and this is far from being the case, for it is by this process of using the available 'clues' within the total situation that what must at first be a general confusion of sounds, gradually becomes ordered, patterned and meaningful. Gradually the child extracts his own meanings, which may draw more from intonation and the accompanying action, than from the words themselves. Amongst stretches of sound for which meaning is yet undifferentiated, meaningful bits, words which are labels for objects, stand out. The ongoing situation helps the child to respond appropriately; thus in time he recognises the repetition of certain phrases as belonging to particular kinds of situations. So the child is helped to distinguish, and then to imitate, words and phrases and to put them together in different combinations dependent upon the meaning which he imposes on the situation and upon the meaning with which these words and phrases are imbued.

After the age of two years the child's speech moves gradually closer to the adult's. His first two- and three-word utterances are made up of elements for which he has been able to extract meaning from the world around him. He will be able to refer to people and objects as he learns to match them with names, and many of his utterances will combine these, and intonation and gestures will fill out the message so that frequently it can be read aright. Other words and short phrases may have developed in a similar way as they appear as a parallel to action.

Learning the meaning of 'no' perhaps marks out an important step. The child will respond to it long before he can produce it for effect himself. The persistent limiting of action which accompanies the adult's 'no' gradually establishes some meaning. The eighteen- or twenty-month-old child can often be heard to murmer 'no' to himself when he pursues activities which have previously earned curtailment. This may not mean that he will cease the activity, but only that this particular sound is generally made by his mother to this particular activity, and he will be expecting her to intervene.

During the period between the child's second and third birthdays, major development takes place. Most children by the age of two-and-a-half will be putting two, and perhaps three words together. Many of the child's attempts at communication are still made by gesture and action, and he is frequently misunderstood. Even when his message is clear there will be many occasions when it will not bring the kind of attention he is wanting. So there will often be frustration, crying and physical protest. Gradually, as he distinguishes the more ambiguous components of speech, and is able to fill out his 'telegraphic' speech, he can convey his meaning more clearly. Not only is he able to give more description as he adds some adjectives to his vocabulary, but because he is able to distinguish different forms of the verb he is able to convey more information about his viewpoint and intention. In fact his speech, during this year, takes on the characteristics of adult speech, although it will show many 'errors.'

During this period, too, he begins to master the use of pronouns. 'It' and 'that' are usually the first, perhaps because they are all symbolic of the action of the pointed finger or nodding the head. The pronouns for persons come later: one of the characteristics of the speech of the young child is that he uses proper names for people where the adult would use a pronoun. Thus he will continue to use his own name:

Johnnie wants the ball. Give it to Johnnie.

Later he will catch on to a general label for the self: 'me.' There is some difficulty for him in isolating the meaning and use of 'I' because of the reversed viewpoint to be taken of the other's reference. Failure to master this may lead us to judge his talk as babyish, even though he has mastered much of the intricacy of adult speech.

By the age of three-and-a-half most children have established speech which is very much like the adult's, although, as we have said, there may be frequent 'mistakes' and some lingering difficulties of articulation. Nevertheless, the major steps have been accomplished and the child's language now becomes an important means of extending his learning.

Children are seen to vary a great deal in the amount of speech they use. Some children seem never to stop chatting, and all their activity is accompanied by speech: others are much more sparing in its use. Such differences are observable in adults too and seem to stem from differences in general personality.

All three-year-old children will not have the kind of ability that Jill and Alison show in the conversation which is quoted at the outset of this chapter. We can be sure, however, that all children will, by the age of three, have established a set of meanings from what they have experienced around them, and it is their own particular set of meanings which provides the basis from which language can develop.

Chapter 2

The Functions of the Child's Language

Our discussion so far has concerned itself mainly with the way in which the young child comes to use language for 'talking.' Children differ in the way in which they learn to speak, in the ability they show in using language, in the rate at which they learn to talk, and in the success they have with articulating sounds. Some differences are important for the teacher to note because they indicate the kind of help that she should try to offer to particular children. When the teacher is listening to what the children are saying to her, or to other children, or to adults in the nursery, or to their mothers, it is possible for her to glean a great deal of information about the stage the child has reached in the development of language.

Perhaps the first thing that will strike her is the readiness of the child to talk to other people. Some children may not speak because of their general shyness, and it is clear that we cannot learn much about the child's command of language until he is sufficiently at home within the classroom to be talking freely.

Mary, for example, was a very shy little girl who, the teacher said, refused to talk at all in school. Indeed, at first she could not play freely. Although she did not cling to her mother, or protest when she was left, it was clear that she needed time to watch and become familiar with life in her new surroundings before she could join in. Each morning she watched, and watched, from the corner where she parted from mother. She responded slowly to the encouragement of the teacher and her assistants, but generally accepted their invitations to accompany them as they moved round the nursery. She would watch other children play and, after two or three weeks, began to take part in activities, watching and imitating other children, but she spoke to no one.

After a time, the teacher talked to Mary's mother about the child's apparent inability to talk in school; she naturally wondered whether Mary was very retarded, since, although some three-year-olds are unwilling to talk much during their first few visits to school, they normally quickly begin to display the kind of skill they have in using language once they are sufficiently relaxed to join in the play activities provided. Many children will suffer a good deal of infringement of their personal rights and comfort in the overwhelming newness of being with so many children and of not knowing quite what is expected of them. So, at first, it was seen by the teacher as quite normal behaviour for Mary to put up with being jostled or pushed by other children with little outward response except a slight shrinking away. Nor was it unusual that she made no verbal protest when, for example, Tommy picked up the spade she had laid down for a moment and took it off to the other end of the sand pit and began digging vigorously with it, watching Mary as though he were surprised that he had been allowed to get away with this trespass so easily.

To begin with, then, Mary's silent behaviour was seen as newness and shyness, but when it persisted beyond the first few days the teacher asked her mother whether Mary had not yet developed much speech. Mary's mother laughed and said jokingly that she could wish that it were so, since Mary never stopped talking at home. Mary was, it seemed, giving them a great deal of information about what happened in the nursery, and it was clear that the mother felt that Mary was a normal talkative child who was finding life in the nursery a source of many interests. 'But,' said Mary's mother, 'she can be very stubborn. She won't talk to strangers at all—even with my sister she shuts up and she sees her several times a year. She makes me feel really stupid when we meet people in the street, or when we go to things at the church. She just won't talk, and whatever I say or do to her only makes her worse.'

This talk with the mother reassured the teacher that Mary's problem was not one of retarded language development, but that the child's difficulties lay in making relationships with other people. Thus she discussed with her assistants and Mary's mother how they might help Mary to settle in to the regime of the nursery without continually demanding that she should talk — demands which she was obviously unable to meet. The teacher felt that once Mary was joining in freely with activities she would gradually be provoked by the attitudes and actions of other children, and also because her own needs would become urgent if her activity was to give her satisfaction. For example, the need for white paint when she had decided to paint a snowman, or when she needed help with cutting material to make a collage picture. Mary, indeed, had problems about using speech, but it was clear that her problems arose not because she had no language through which to communicate, but because she had difficulty in finding a relationship with other people in which she felt able to express herself.

Some children, like Peter, will not respond readily to the teacher or other adults, but can be observed to talk with brothers and sisters or with other children. Again, by observation the teacher can discover that although Peter does not respond to her talk, he nevertheless has established a good deal of language which he uses with other children. Such observation helps the teacher to decide upon a course of action which first aims at changing attitudes. It may be that Peter comes from a home where he has learned to use language in very restricted ways, which do not include responding to the kind of use of language which the teacher employs, for example, giving explanations to questions, or reasons for making particular demands. This is a problem to which we shall return.

It is clear that the teacher's only way of making some assessment of the skill the child has in using language is to listen closely when the child is talking. If the child's ability to use language is to be fully revealed, then the more frequently the teacher listens to him in a number of different kinds of situation, the more likely is she to observe his full repertoire of skills.

But what would the teacher listen for? Having noted the immaturity of the child's speech and his mistakes, and his problems of articulation, what more can she recognise about the child's skill in using language? To help us identify different kinds of skill in using language it would perhaps be useful to look at the recorded speech of some three-year-olds and examine the purposes for which they seem to use language. The following extract is taken from a recording of two three-year-olds as they played together with a number of motor cars and lorries:

Jimmie: Going on there brr-brr—off to Morecambe.
Two cars—brr-brr—on there—go on there.
Now that one brr—come on here—oo! bump!
Out of the way. Put that on—now, brr —.

Tom is watching Jimmie, he picks up the car and Jimmie is startled.

Jimmie: Give me that car. That one's mine.
Tom: No—no. I want it. You can have that one—there.
Jimmie: All right—brr-brr—pushing it on the road now.
Tom: Get out—get out of the way.
It's going to crash.
Jimmie: Right—right.
Watch—watch me. Brr—brr—it's there—crash!
Tom: It did—it did bang crash.
Again—do it again.
Jimmie: Yes—right.
Ready—ready Tom.
Send yours on here.

Peter watches and makes as though to intervene and pick up Tom's car.

Tom: Hey, Pete—mind—mind out of the way.
No, go away.
Me and Jimmie doing this—not you—not you.

This talk can be seen to serve several functions. First and foremost, perhaps, it is maintaining a working relationship between the two little boys. They are for the most part playing side-by-side and their speech serves to keep them in touch with each other, perhaps just indicating that each is aware of the other's presence and that they're quite content to be near each other. In a way, each provides an audience for the other: 'Watch—watch me!'

Obviously the speech here has a social purpose. Speech in any case is a social act, that is, it takes place between people: we would not learn to speak at all unless there were someone to listen and respond to our early efforts. It is true that we often hear the child between three and six talking as though to himself; even though others are near he seems oblivious of their presence, or sometimes he may seem aware of them although he does not appear to address his speech to them. In a way, it seems that often the young child treats himself as the audience and parallels his activities with a running commentary. This seems to be the case at the beginning of this reported episode. Jimmie, although he has been playing with and alongside Tom for quite a while, appears to have forgotten Tom's presence and uses speech almost as though he is monitoring his own actions. Indeed in the first section his speech is mostly a parallel of his action:

Going on there brr-brr—off to Morecambe.
Two cars—brr-brr—on there—go on there.
Now that one brr—come on here—oo! Bump!
Out of the way. Put that on—now brr.

The only element of speech which is not a parallel of some part of the ongoing concrete situation is his reference to Morecambe as a place to be off to. We can see that speech is functioning here as an accompaniment to Jimmie's play, a reflection to himself of his activity, perhaps directing his own attention to what he is doing.

There is clearly a change in the function of the utterances which follow. Jimmie becomes aware of Tom's presence. Tom threatens Jimmie's activity by picking up one of Jimmie's cars. Jimmie now uses speech to assert his rights, to protect his property and Tom employs speech to assert his claim, but maintains the working relationship between the two of them by compensating Jimmie with a different car:

Jimmie: Give me that car. That one's mine.
Tom: No-no, I want it. You can have that one there.

At this point Tom has made a decision not to return Jimmie's car, but to offer him something else. Tom is not always successful in maintaining social relationships with other children. With another child, Mark, for example who is older and bigger and confident in his own strength and status, Tom might have acted and spoken differently, perhaps giving way saying 'All right I'll have the blue car then.' But on this occasion he has judged the situation well. Jimmie does not challenge Tom's authority further but accepts the alternative Tom offers:

Jimmie: All right—brr-brr—pushing it on the road now.

Jimmie might, of course, have sought the help of an adult to maintain his rights to the car. Both children in a way have made a series of decisions. Tom decides to hold on to the car, but to compensate Jimmie for the loss; Jimmie decides to accept the offer and between them the children have maintained the pleasure of playing with and alongside each other. Their speech offered the means of communicating their decisions to each other. Language served the function of maintaining the social relationships between the two. But in doing so, it should be noted that the child is learning to make judgements about people and their likely reactions, in other words, to take the other's point of view, an activity which draws upon his intellect.

Having successfully maintained the play relationship, language is then employed to promote the play, even to achieve co-operation between themselves. Each instructs the other to perform some action, each expresses agreement with the intended action:

Tom: Get out—get out of the way.
          It's going to crash.
Jimmie: Right—right.
          Watch—watch me. Brr-brr—it's there—crash!
Tom: It did—it did bang crash.
          Again—do it again.

Again, the intellect is at work making judgements about the messages coming from the other, and sending off new messages which have the intention of achieving the crash climax. Through pitch and intonation the children signal their enjoyment to each other. The activity gives them pleasure: using speech is not only a way of fending off misunderstanding, but of securing agreement of intention. Towards the end we see that speech serves the purpose of defending the rights of Tom and Jimmie against the threat which Peter's presence and action suggest exists:

Tom: Hey Pete—mind out of the way.
         No—go away.
         Me and Jimmie doing this—not you—not you.

In this short record we can see that language functions for the child in several ways:

1   To maintain a working together relationship between the two little boys.
2   To express intentions about actions to each other.
3   To secure co-operation and co-ordinate action.
4   To defend each child's rights of property and status, including threatening or abusing the other.
5   To monitor the child's own activity.

So using language, even at this age is a pretty complicated business, but we take the fact that we speak, and that children learn to talk at an early age, so much for granted that as teachers, if we overheard a conversation like the above, we would remark on its poverty of expression and its lack of complexity in structure, rather than on the complexity of the mental activity which makes it possible.

Let us listen to another group of children who are playing together in much the same way as Tom and Jimmie. Here are two little boys, Mark and John, and they too have taken up the cars and are busy maintaining a similar working relationship. They are also both three years old:

Mark: That's my red car John.
John: But it isn't really.
Mark: Well—I was playing with it—I had it first.

John: Oh—well—which shall I have then?
I'm going to have the blue one and I'm going to race it.

Mark: Mine's racing too—round it goes.

John: Push your car faster Mark, like this. Wow—wow—mine's going fast as anything—as anything and fast as a train.

Mark: Mine's going fast as a rocket—whoosh.

John: Watch out Mark—my car's coming fast—I think there'll be a crash—make yours come to mine.

Mark: Yes there will be a big crash—mine's coming—watch out—brr—there—there crash.

John: Oh an accident, an accident—my car's on fire.

Mark: Fetch the fire engine—the cars are burning all up.

John: And the people are getting all burnt up too.

He takes up a lorry and makes fire engine noises.

John: Er-er Er-er—here's the fire engine coming.

Mark: Bring it here John, by the cars—put the water on.

John: Get out the thingummy—the long thing you know.

Mark: Yes—woosh—all water going on the fire.
Er-er—the ambulance is coming to take the people to hospital.

The speech in this episode has a different quality from the previous one although the language functions in a similar way to maintain the working relationship between the two. There is a threat to the child's possession, but in this case the child brings an argument to his defence—he has evidence to show that he has a claim to the car as his. John might not have accepted this argument but he maintains Mark's goodwill by accepting this as good reason, although he allows himself to point out that actual ownership is not Mark's, although he accepts Mark's claim to it at this point:

Mark: That's my red car John.

John: But it isn't really.

Mark: Well—I was playing with it—I had it first.

John: Oh—well—which shall I have then?

In this case the use of language has allowed argument or reasoning to play a part in resolving the problem. Although there is in both episodes a social relationship to be maintained, and language serves to accomplish this, judgements at an intellectual level have to be made about how best to resolve the situation. The second example demonstrates a new entity, the strengthening of a social relationship through reasoning expressed and communicated through speech.

Mark and John start off on a game very similar to that played by Tom and Jimmie, but again there is a different quality entering in. There is the communication of intended action, there is direction of one's own, and the other's actions, there is co-operation and co-ordination to achieve a particular end, the crash:

John: I'm going to have the blue one and I'm going to race it.
Mark: Mine's racing too—round it goes.
John: Push your car faster Mark, like this. Wow—wow—mine's going fast as anything—as anything and fast as a train.
Mark: Mine's going fast as a rocket—whoosh —.
John: Watch out Mark—my car's coming fast—I think there'll be a crash—make yours come to mine.
Mark: Yes there will be a crash—and mine's coming—watch out—brr—there—there crash.

But there is a striking difference between the two conversations due mainly to the extent to which both Mark and John use language in order to bring into their play information about things which lie outside the present situation. The idea of racing is introduced, comparison of speed leads to the comparing of the speed of cars, trains and rockets, there is prediction of the outcome of their present action.

Up to this point the language has had a close link with the reality of the on-going situation, although it is clear that the cars have become symbols for real cars, as was also the case in Jimmie and Tom's play. But then quite a different element enters:

John: An accident, an accident—my car's on fire.
Mark: Fetch the fire engine—the cars are all burning up.

From this point on, the language used sets up the scene, there is no real fire, no fire engine (a lorry is made to become a fire engine), no people and not even any material used symbolically for people, and no ambulance. Noises represent fire engine and ambulance, and the scene of the fire and the race to the hospital are entirely dependent on the language used by the children for evidence of their presence:

John: And the people are getting all burnt up too.
            Er-er Er-er—here's the fire engine coming.
Mark: Bring it here John, by the cars—put the water on.
John: Get out the thingummy—the long thing—you know.
Mark: Yes—woosh—all water going on the fire.
            Er-er—the ambulance is coming to take the people to hospital.

The children react to the language as though the scene it sets up were a reality. We are not saying that the children react to the fantasy as they would to the actuality, but that their behaviour is a response to the scene set up by language and not just to the scene as it exists in concrete, that is, to blue and red toy cars on the floor.

We can see in this extract examples of several other functions that language performs. Perhaps the most important asset language brings is that it allows us to exchange information about objects, people, incidents, and events, which are not to be observed at the time of speaking. Language allows us to recall things which are past, or remote from us. It allows us to re-examine situations which may never recur or to rehearse and examine the possibilities of an event before it occurs. It allows the child to build up a fantasy structure based on recalled information and knowledge, and to live through imagined episodes which he might never meet in reality.

Let us return to more of Mark and John's conversation. They are looking at a shoe box and discussing its suitability for making a garage:

Mark: Well, you know, garages have to have doors.
John: Sometimes they don't.
Mark: Garages have to have doors that will open and shut.
John: My grandad has one and he puts his car in and that hasn't doors.
Mark: But a garage has doors—and you lock the door so nobody can take it—the car you see.
John: My grandad has a car thing and it hasn't doors on. It just keeps the rain off you.
Mark: Oh—well—shall we make a garage or a car thing like your grandad's?
John: Well, I don't know how to put doors on.
Mark: I would think of glue or pins or something like that.
John: No—put it this way up see—and cut it.
Mark: Yes, that might be all right.
John: Right—Mark—right—I'll get the scissors.

Here we see further uses for language in addition to some we have already referred to. Without doubt these two little boys speak in such a way as to maintain their good working relationship—considering each other's point of view, for example:

Shall we make?
I don't know how to put doors on.
That might be all right.

But there is little here that reflects action, in fact it has about it a very adult-like air of discussion. The question is how to make a garage. The shoe box provides an anchor in the present. Both boys use language to express information about past experience which has some relevance for the present problem. Mark's first statement: 'Well you know, garages have to have doors' is not accepted by John as a valid conclusion; he has seen evidence to the contrary, but his 'Sometimes they don't' acknowledges that they often do have doors. Both little boys then endeavour to be more explicit in order to establish their own case:

Mark: Garages have to have doors that will open and shut.

He cannot envisage a garage without doors for letting the cars in and out; he persists with his argument:

> Mark: But a garage has doors—and you lock the door so nobody can take it—the car you see.

Clearly Mark has a very full notion of the purpose for which a garage serves. But John also must be more explicit; his case is also a valid one and he struggles to convey to Mark the way in which a garage without doors will work.

> John: My grandad has one and he puts his car in and that hasn't doors.
> John: My grandad has a car thing and it hasn't doors on. It just keeps the rain off you.

Both children here make an effort to reveal to each other the meaning which each attaches to 'garage.' Through the sharing of knowledge perhaps each extends his own meaning. John is presented with the conflict between Mark's argument that garages have to have doors so that cars can be locked up and kept safe, and his own knowledge about his grandfather's car port. Perhaps his later reference to a 'car thing' suggests that he has recognised what the essential characteristics of a garage are, and that his grandfather's does not qualify as a garage.

Mark, on the other hand, concedes that John has a point, that it is possible to have somewhere to put a car that does not have doors. The argument in fact demonstrates the way in which even the young child's meanings can be modified by means of a transaction through the use of language. Mark demonstrates very clearly his acceptance of the possibility presented by John although preserving the distinction between 'a garage' and 'a car thing.' He resolves the slight conflict of views:

> Mark: Oh—well—shall we make a garage or a car thing like your grandad's?

In the remainder of the conversation we see the children searching for a solution to their problem of construction. John's

'I don't know how to' and Mark's 'I would think of' both suggest serious efforts to reflect on the problem. They see possibilities, they survey alternatives and together arrive at a decision. This kind of linguistic activity seems to support the view that these children have already learned to analyse, to examine, to select, and to discriminate. Such mental activities form the basis for an intelligent appraisal of the world. Their language reflects an awareness of the appropriateness of the slight differences in meaning which choice from a number of alternative forms of expression through language makes possible. The child who is able to use language in this way demonstrates sensitivity not only to the features and detail of the physical world around him, but also to the feelings of the people with whom he communicates: he has become aware of the importance of choosing language which supports an appropriate relationship between himself and his listener: his choice of language will be influenced not only by the message that he is wanting to convey but also by his recognition of the relationship which exists between himself and the person to whom he speaks.

Consider for a moment the messages given by two five-year-old boys to their teacher:

Jimmie: Not got to have my milk.
Teacher: Why not Jimmie?
Jimmie: My mum says I haven't to.

And the following:

Michael: Could I stay inside today?
Teacher: Why don't you want to go out Michael?
Michael: I've got a cold you see.
           It makes me cough outside 'cos it's very cold.

These two children have given very similar basic messages: 'I'm not to drink my milk today' and 'I'm not to go outside today.'

The first is a bald statement which makes no attempt to reconcile the rival authorities of parent and teacher. It makes no attempt to anticipate the effect the form in which the message is cast might have on the teacher. The same form would probably be used to convey the information to another child.

The second message, on the other hand, is sensitive to the teacher's authority and the language selected makes no challenge to it. Michael selects a question form, with a degree of tentativeness in 'Could I?' and the teacher's reaction as listener has been anticipated.

Both children are asked to explain their reason for the requests. Jimmie gives his mother's authority, she says so, but again he fails to communicate the reason why mother says he must not have milk, that is he is not feeling too well and he may not be able to tolerate milk today.

Michael, on the other hand, expects to give a logical explanation. It is his mother's request he is conveying, but he knows that mother has reasons for making the request and he tries to present them to the teacher in a cause-effect kind of argument. This is the kind of explanation the teacher expects and Michael is sensitive to her expectancy. To his friend in the playground he might have said 'I've not to play out today,' but he intuitively knows that the message couched in these terms is not an appropriate form to offer to the teacher.

The child, we see, even at this early age, uses language in an effort to manipulate people and influence their decisions: having a repertoire of a number of possible ways of expressing messages makes it possible for the child to gain some control, not only over his own explorations of the variety of experiences the world can offer him, but also over those people who inhabit his world. Language functions for the child as a means of influencing the attitudes and actions of other people towards himself.

We have here considered briefly the functions of the young child's use of language. Although we have quoted only a few examples to illustrate the points we have tried to make, it is clear that all children have already learned to use language for a number of different purposes by the time they are coming to nursery school. From the few examples given it can be seen that some functions appear to demand and reflect more complex mental activity than others. Monitoring, or commenting upon the present concrete scene, for example, seems to be one of the simpler functions compared with, for example, explaining, or reasoning about the relationships which might be seen to exist between the various components of that scene. Here are the responses of some five-year-old children as they looked at a scene which showed a family in the kitchen:

Tom: There's a man and a lady.
There's a little girl and that's a boy.
Look, there's a pussy and it's on the drawer.
And there's a table and a sink.

Here Tommy is doing little more than placing labels on the several components of the scene.

Mark, on the other hand, looks at the scene and apparently takes account of particular details, and seeks to find a satisfactory account of the scene as a whole.

Mark: Well—it's a family in the kitchen, I think. I think they've just had their breakfast, because the daddy's still sitting at the table reading the newspaper.
And I think the little girl's helping the mummy to do the washing up, because she's doing something at the sink, isn't she? I don't know what the little boy's doing—perhaps he's telling the cat to get down from there—it shouldn't be on the sideboard should it?

This second example suggests that Mark has learned to look for structure and relationships: he is interpreting the whole scene. In a way he has taken the request from the teacher to 'tell me all about what you can see in the picture' as a problem which he has set about solving. He does not just see a man and a table and a newspaper, but sees the way in which they are connected as important. The man is sitting at a table reading a newspaper —but why should he be doing that? For Mark the answer is that this is an activity which is usual at the breakfast table. Looking at the rest of the scene he perhaps sees the position of the girl and the woman and their nearness to the sink as further evidence which supports his 'after breakfast' solution. His whole inclination seems to be to establish a meaning and explanation for the whole scene.

The mental activity reflected in Mark's response would seem to be more complex than that of Tom's labelling or identifying response, and perhaps their use of language may reflect important differences in their thinking. The more complex mental activity seems likely to require more complexity in the language used to express it. There is the use of 'because' which permits him to present evidence for his judgements. The use of 'I think,' and 'perhaps' shows that he is aware that there may be other explanations. Unlike Tom's use of unconnected items, Mark shows his awareness of relatedness or connectedness between people, things and actions, for example, 'daddy's still sitting at the table reading the newspaper' and 'the little girl's helping the mummy to do the washing-up because she's doing something at the sink.'

Mark also shows that he structures the several components of the scene into a meaningful whole. He must, like Tom, see the individual people, the pieces of furniture, but unlike Tom he does not first list them but gathers them together to produce a total structure which they form together 'a family in the kitchen.' In this way he imposes a meaning upon the scene which Tom fails to express through his language.

These examples illustrate that it is the meaning which his experiences have for the child which give rise to the use of different forms of language. Where meaning is more complex, its adequate expression demands a complex use of language and this is reflected in the child's talking. Most children, when they come to nursery school are using a great deal of talk, but they may not be using it to express the same kind of complexity of meaning.

All young children seem to use language often for maintaining or promoting their own self interest in an effort as it were to succeed both at the physical and psychological level. Thus 'I want,' 'Give me,' 'Can I have?' 'Stop it,' 'That's mine,' 'You're naughty,' 'Go away,' 'Get off,' 'Look at me,' 'Aren't I clever?' 'Watch me jump,' can be observed. They also seem to use a great deal of speech for commenting both on the ongoing scene and on their own actions.

Some children, even by the age of three, are beginning to use language to express complex meaning, as we can see from some of the examples given in this and the earlier chapter. The language of other children, however, seems to refer only to the immediate scene and the more complex uses seem to be absent. Some reasons for such observed differences in children's talk are explored in the next chapter.

Chapter 3

Talk in the Home

It is quite clear that there are great differences between children in their ability to use language and to express their ideas effectively in speech. The teacher will generally see two possible explanations for these differences: differences in intelligence, and differences in home background. The first explanation, of course, is well known: tests of verbal ability do distinguish between children in much the same way as other kinds of intelligence tests as a general rule. The question which might be asked, however, and to which so far there seems to be no clear answer, is whether verbal skill is merely the reflection of intelligence or whether in some way verbal skill promotes the development of intelligence. It would seem likely that both of these are true and that the child's intelligence and developing verbal skill support and extend each other.

The second explanation, that it is the child's home experience that is responsible for differences in children's ability to use language, would seem to be an obvious one, but the cause may not be that which is often put forward, that a child's inability to use language adequately is because his parents do not talk to him enough. It is usually the mother that is cited as the culprit as the young child spends most of his day in her company. To what extent are we right in making this judgement? It is true that the child learns to use language during the years when home provides his experience almost entirely. Even after the child comes to school he still spends the major part of his time at home, or out with playmates who live in his immediate neighbourhood. So without a doubt we can say that the child's home experience is the source of his early learning about language, and persists as the main influence for many years.

It is also true that if mothers do not talk with their children speech is not likely to develop normally unless some other person provides adequate stimulation. Mothers who do not talk to their children are, in fact, neglecting their children, although this may not be their intention. A young mother confessed that she had not known that her first baby *needed* company until her second baby began to talk. She had not played with her older child or talked to her much whilst she was tiny, but had always kept her well-fed and clean. This older child had been tucked up in her cot or pram for the major part of the day and, as she grew older, was left to play by herself in her playpen. The parents had wondered why this child had not begun to speak at an age when the children of their friends began to utter their first words. This little girl, a rather quiet, undemanding child, was very much retarded until the second baby, of a more robust temperament, began to demand attention. The mother talked to her second child as she responded to her demandingness and the older child was drawn into this experience and also began to talk during this period. Only then did the mother realise why the first baby had been so late in learning to talk, whilst her second baby learned with such ease.

More often, perhaps, such neglect will be a reflection of the mother's rejection of the child and the child will have serious emotional problems. Such children may also be retarded in speech, although not necessarily so, for the mother's rejection may find expression through talking and the child will thus have an adequate experience of language although the feelings which are expressed may be instrumental in damaging his view of himself, of other people and of the world in general.

But usually it is not this kind of inadequacy to which a teacher refers when she speaks of the child whom she feels is handicapped by his home experiences. Generally the children referred to come from homes where parents have themselves benefited little from education, and who expect little for their children from education. Children from such homes may not respond in a normal way to the teacher's requests or be able to offer explanations or to express their needs adequately or even to make appropriate comments on what they see happening in school. Naturally the teacher will feel that it is the home that is at fault and will tend to assume that it is because the child has not experienced much use of language in his home.

The teacher is right in that the child has not experienced talk used in the way, or for the purposes which teachers see to be important. The mothers and families of these children may use language just as much as others but the attitudes which are expressed through speech, and the attitudes towards the use of language and the purposes for which language is used may be very different from the teacher's own practice. Because of his experiences the child has already formed different expectations about how language is used, expectations which have been learned through the regular practices of his home. The teacher on the other hand has an expectancy about how children should use language, which is based on personal experience of using language. When the teacher says that the child has no language this may be true to the extent that the child has learned to expect adults to use language in certain ways; if the adult does not meet that expectation then he is at a loss, and fails to make a response which the teacher sees as appropriate or adequate.

There are other children who, even by the age of three, have already learned to use language in a very adult manner. They can initiate conversation, ask questions, give suitable answers, and generally use language for getting along with their teachers and for exploring and examining the situations they find within school. How can such different attitudes and skill in using language develop? What has happened to the child during these early years to cause such differences of behaviour to be established.

All mothers are concerned with the behaviour of their young children; they want their children to fit into the family routine, to get on well with the rest of the family, and with friends and neighbours, and to become physically independent of mother as quickly as possible. Much of the talk that the child is involved in whilst he is learning to use language is concerned with the way of life of the family, what the family expects of its children, the interests of the members of the family and their attitudes to each other. The situations in which he is involved in talk with his parents and brothers and sisters provide the need and the example which urge him into learning to take part in the talking.

Perhaps looking at some conversations between two mothers and their three-year-old sons, will help us to make our point more clearly.

First of all we will look at three-year-old Jimmie and his mother talking. These examples are typical of many incidents which were recorded in the course of one day.

1 Mother and Jimmie are in the kitchen. She is finishing washing up the breakfast things and Jimmie is inspecting the electric kettle:

Mother: Hey, Jimmie, what're you up to now? Where are you? Good heavens—what next!

Mother slaps him and the kettle is roughly pulled away.

Mother: Haven't I told you not to touch the kettle? You do as I say or you'll get hurt. Don't you climb up there again—and don't touch the kettle, see!
No don't cry—there—don't cry—Oh come on you baby—you're not hurt now.
Come on—give us a cuddle and a kiss—you're my big boy—but do as I say—be a good boy.

Mother puts Jimmie down on a chair at the table. He looks at the picture on the outside of the cereal packet.

Jimmie: What's that?
Mother: It's a submarine.
Hey—mind your feet—sit properly.
Jimmie: What's it do?
Mother: Did you hear me—get your feet off the chair.
Jimmie: What's that thing do?
Mother: What thing—oh that—it's a submarine. Sit on that chair properly, or else go out to play.

2 Later in the day; Jimmie is playing with the baby's rattle:

Mother: Hey don't do that—give it back to her—it's hers. Do you hear—give Michele her rattle. You don't want a rattle do you? You're not a baby are you? Are you? You're a big boy—you don't want a rattle. See—just give her it like I say.

Jimmie: I want it. I want one.

Mother: No you don't—that's for baby.
Where's your car?

3 Mother has put the baby to bed and has tidied the living-room. Jimmie is lying on the floor, obviously tired:

Mother: Time you were in bed.

Jimmie: No—not go to bed.

Mother: Now no nonsense, time for little boys to go to bed.

Jimmie: No—no—not go bed.

He wriggles and kicks.

Mother: Don't say no to me.
Your dad'll see to you
—Come on—do as I say.

Jimmie gets up and stamps.

Jimmie: Sweetie—me want sweetie.

Mother: There you are again.
Watch that paddy now.
Come on—be a good boy now —
Let's get your things off.

Jimmie: Want sweetie—want sweetie.

Mother: You're a proper terror you are. What will your dad say? Come on—get your things off—a sweetie when you're ready if I can find one. Oh, you're tired aren't you?
Come on I'll carry you up.

Jimmie snuggles into his mother's arms and she carries him to bed.

This final conversation was recorded when Jimmie was five.

4 Mother and visitor are standing by the kitchen door. The baby is in her pram and Jimmie is sitting on a patch of grass. The visitor has asked whether Jimmie is like any of the older children in the family:

Mother: No not him—he's the wick* one of the family—
never still, wants to know what's going on. Right
little nosey parker he is. The others are not like
that—more easy like—satisfied with what you say.
He just keeps on pestering—drives me crazy
sometimes.

Jimmie comes up to mother, hand clenched.

Jimmie: Look—look what I've found.
Mother: Just look at your hands—black bright aren't they?
Jimmie: Look at this thing—this ladybird—look it's right
little.
Mother: Go wash your hands now—just look at the colour
of them.
Jimmie: It's a ladybird. I want to keep it.
Mother: Go wash your hands now—do as I say—and put
that thing down. Let it go—do you hear.
Jimmie: I want it—I want to keep it.
Mother: Whatever next. Go wash your hands and don't
make a mess. You can have a biscuit then.

These examples may not be fully representative of all the talk
that goes on between Jimmie and his mother, but they are
representative of other occasions on which recordings were
made. Jimmie's mother may use other kinds of talk with Jimmie
even though it was not observed, but to help us to make our
point, let us assume that she does not. If these examples were
typical of all Jimmie's experience of talk in the home what could
we expect Jimmie to be learning?

First of all, it is made quite clear to him what is expected of
him in matters of cleanliness; he mustn't roll on the floor and
get dirty and he must wash his hands when they are dirty. There
are also certain behaviours which he must avoid, touching the
kettle, climbing on to the kitchen table, and putting his feet on
the chair. Jimmie is also made very much aware of what is
inappropriate or appropriate behaviour for a boy of his age; he
mustn't cry—only babies cry and he's a big boy; he mustn't
play with the rattle—only babies play with rattles; he must go
to bed when mother tells him; he must not say no to his mother;

* Wick=quick, lively.

he must be a good boy and do as mother says. Jimmie might also learn that Dad is the final authority.

Much of Jimmie's mother's talk is concerned with persuading Jimmie to be a 'good little boy'; she often emphasises the position of each member of the family and the behaviour expected of each. Jimmie's mother is trying to impose on Jimmie ways of behaving which are considered appropriate for him as the little (or big) boy of the family, but she does little to help him understand why such behaviour is required from him. On the one occasion where such an explanation is given it remains ambiguous: 'Don't touch the kettle or you'll get hurt.' Jimmie may be left uncertain as to whether he will be hurt by the kettle or hurt by mother.

Although Jimmie is not being helped to understand why mother does not want him to behave in certain ways, perhaps he is learning other things. Jimmie opens up opportunities for information to be given to him but all are turned aside by mother because she is entirely concerned with his behaviour. His question, 'What's it do?' is ignored. His 'Look, I've found a ladybird' is met with a demand for him to wash his hands. If this is typical of the mother's responses to Jimmie's questions we might expect that Jimmie will learn not to look for answers, and perhaps that he will learn not to ask questions since they are rarely rewarded by bringing him the information he seeks. Jimmie's mother talks to him a great deal but mainly in order to inform Jimmie about the way he must behave: she seems to be unaware of the opportunities for other kinds of talk which Jimmie's curiosity produces.

If the above examples really are typical of the way in which speech is used in Jimmie's home, what might we expect him *not* to learn during the years in which he is learning to talk? It is clear that Jimmie is certainly not learning that the adult can be a source of interesting information. Although he is learning to look to the adult for instruction as to how he must behave, he is not learning the reasons which lie behind such demands: he is not learning the principles by which he can judge and control his own behaviour. He is learning to look to the adult to control him, and when no adult is there to refer to, we should not be surprised to find that he behaves quite differently.

There is no evidence to suggest that Jimmie's mother is not caring for him well: Jimmie is well nourished and he is quite adequately clothed and his general physical needs are provided for. There is plenty of evidence to show that Jimmie is well loved. Much of this attitude of care and affection is communicated to Jimmie by the way in which his mother takes hold of him, or touches him, by the warmth in her voice, often in spite of the scolding nature of the words she uses, and by the physical comfort she offers him, the sweets and the biscuits.

Nor is there any evidence to suggest that Jimmie's mother does not talk to him much. In fact, quite the reverse is the case, she does talk to him a great deal when he is in the house with her. Jimmie, however, spends considerable time outside his home even at the age of three. Before attending the nursery, he spent a good deal of time on fine days out in the cul-de-sac on to which his home faces, playing with the young children from the neighbouring houses. He is allowed to wander with his playmates round the near-by roads of the housing estate. His mother feels that there is not much threat from traffic and that it is good for children to be out playing with their friends. So there are parts of the day when Jimmie is well beyond the reach of his mother's voice, but when he is at home with her there is no doubt that she talks to him a good deal.

Is Jimmie's teacher wrong, then, when she says that Jimmie's home is responsible for his inability to use language adequately when he comes to nursery school? Before we answer this question, let us see how another mother talks with her three-year-old son, Mark.

Mark and his little sister Julie are playing on the floor. He is looking through a box of toy vehicles. He stops to examine a toy lorry. Their mother is sitting on a low chair beside them, knitting as she watches and talks with them:

Mark: What's this funny thing for?
Mother: Let me look—oh yes, see it's a hook. Can you find something that will fasten on behind the lorry?

Mark: Yes—I see—well it might be a breakdown one couldn't it?

Mother: Oh, do you think so? What are breakdown lorries like?—do you remember?

Mark: I know—I know—'cos I saw one. At Grannie's I saw one. It's not a breakdown thing—it hasn't got a big thing that pulls up.

Mother: A big thing? You mean the crane do you—that lifts the car up?

Mark: Yes, it lifts it up like this—off the ground to pull the car—the accident one you see.

Mother: And isn't this a breakdown lorry then?

Mark: No, no—it's only a hook. It's for pulling I think.

Mother: I wonder what it might pull.

Mark: I'm looking—perhaps a cart or a thing behind, like this.

Mother: You mean a trailer.

Mark: Yes, Julie give me that—I want to fasten it on.

Mark pulls away the trailer from Julie—Julie begins to protest.

Mother: Oh, that wasn't kind Mark, was it? Julie was playing with it. She doesn't like you taking it like that. You should have asked her if she would change for something else. Julie you have the fire engine instead.

Mark: She's a baby isn't she?

Mother: Would you like me to take your lorry now?

Mark: No you can't.

Mother: No—well—Julie doesn't like it either—but she's all right now. What does the fire engine say Julie?

Julie makes a noise and Mark joins in laughing with his baby sister.

This conversation is very different in several ways from those we have quoted between Jimmie and his mother. Let us look at the reported episodes to see how differently their mothers respond to their questions.

Jimmie shows interest in the picture of a submarine on a

breakfast cereal packet (page 31). He asks his mother 'What's that?' His mother responds by naming the object as a submarine but immediately switches her attention to Jimmie's behaviour: 'Mind your feet—sit properly.' Jimmie persists with his search for understanding 'What's it do?' he questions. His mother entirely ignores his question and continues to instruct him about the way to sit on a chair.

Each time Jimmie makes an opportunity for his mother to help him to extend his understanding, his mother responds by referring to something which is in her mind, and is meaningful to her. She seems unaware of Jimmie's need, and demand, for additional meaning. Rarely is meaning held in common by the two of them: their talk is seen to follow separate paths and Jimmie's mother really does not talk *with* Jimmie but *at* Jimmie.

In a later episode (page 33) we see an even clearer example of the failure to start with Jimmie's meaning. 'Look what I've found' he says with a thrill of excitement in his voice, but his mother fails to follow the focus of Jimmie's attention and communicate with him at the level at which this experience has meaning for him. Her attention is on Jimmie's dirty hands. Here lies meaning for her at this moment and Jimmie's need is not recognised. But Jimmie persists, holding on to his own meaning 'This ladybird—it's right little!' But his mother seems unable to switch her attention from what is important to her, to consider that which is important to Jimmie and his invitations to talk are dismissed. We see that Jimmie and his mother never seem to hold a conversation in which meanings are exchanged and at times extended. The episode consists of two monologues which proceed without ever touching on a common core of meaning which would provide the impetus towards the extension of knowledge and understanding.

Let us now look at a comparable episode between Mark and his mother (page 35). Mark approaches his mother with 'What's this funny thing for?' Immediately his mother centres on what is meaningful for Mark: 'See it is a hook' she says and proceeds to help Mark to think about the function of a hook. Mark goes on 'It might be a breakdown lorry' and this continues his flow of thought: his mother supports this continuation of ideas by helping him to remember a breakdown lorry he has seen and compare it with the present vehicle. He gives his eye to the detail; he refines his definition.

In answering Mark's questions, his mother responds in such a way as to encourage him to go on thinking about the problem. She invites him to recall past experiences in order to understand the new one. She helps him to clarify his memory and gives him the name for 'the big thing which lifts up'—so increasing his vocabulary. She indicates to Mark that there may be a number of possible solutions, 'I wonder what it might pull.'

We can see that Mark's mother is quite effectively encouraging Mark (and the younger child too is experiencing all this reasoning and informative talk, even though she may not yet understand it all) to use language for the exploration of past and immediate experiences and to anticipate possible actions and solutions to problems.

And so this conversation goes on, with his mother each time taking Mark's meaning as the starting point and then leading him in some way to an extension of his understanding.

Mark snatches a lorry from Julie and she cries. Now his mother shows her disapproval clearly and suggests an alternative acceptable behaviour. When Mark refers to Julie as a baby his mother challenges his behaviour and helps him to realise how Julie feels. Mark protests that he doesn't like this—nor does Julie, persists his mother, whilst the possibility that he might be led to recognise a general principle exists.

Mark's mother shows great skill in this episode in meeting Mark at a point within his own thinking and interest. She starts with the idea that Mark has just expressed, then she helps him to extend his understanding of his own behaviour towards Julie, and leads him towards condemning his behaviour towards Julie. At the age of three he is hardly able to embrace this meaning, but we can see that by such strategies his mother will gradually lead him to recognise the principle that the rights of others must be always respected. In this way she helps him to establish routes by which meaning can be generalised from one situation to another and be instrumental in developing understanding at a deeper level.

If the above example is typical of only a part of Mark's experience in using language, we can see that he is likely to be developing a view of the role of the adult which is quite different from Jimmie's. The adult, for Mark, is one who offers information, who invites thought and discussion, who reflects his behaviour back to him, inviting him to participate in the control of his own behaviour.

He learns that to ask questions brings information, to try to solve problems brings approval, and that language makes past experience live again. His attitudes towards adults, towards his own behaviour and towards using language, are quite different from the attitudes which Jimmie might be expected to be forming as the result of his experiences of talk with his mother.

The examples quoted are real enough, but of course it is impossible to record the whole of a child's experiences of talking at home. We can only use such examples to give us some insight into the way in which the child's experiences might account for the fostering of certain attitudes and the development of particular skills. Different environments, which employ language differently, seem likely to account for some of the differences in children's ability to communicate through language. Even by the time the child is three years old, living in a particular kind of environment will already have had a marked effect.

Chapter 4

Talk in School

When children come to school we see differences in the way in which they respond to the teacher's talk and to the talk of other children. What many have learnt to do with language at home will help them to adjust to this new experience. There are others who will be at great disadvantage because of the way in which they learnt to use language at home.

Let us look again at Jimmie, and the problems which he meets during his first weeks in the nursery class attached to an infants' school: he is now just turned four years old.

His teacher is very warm and friendly, as is her assistant, and both are eager to do their best for all the children. They have known Jimmie's family for several years, and four older brothers and a sister have passed through the class.

> If he's anything like the others (says his teacher) he'll be a bit wild. They take advantage if you're not careful. Lively enough, you know, but not very bright, at least only in a practical way and if they're interested. It's difficult to get them to concentrate—as for reading—none of them have managed to get past book one before they've left for the juniors. It's that sort of home—happy enough, no physical neglect you know—but they're not talked to much I expect and they let them run wild. But basically they're all nice children—and I expect Jimmie will be the same.

It is only natural for the teacher to take this view; this is what her experience of the family seems to indicate; this is how she interprets what she has seen. Yet it is obvious that some of her assumptions are wrong; it is clear that Jimmie hears a lot of talk and it is also clear that within the home, at least, he is controlled very firmly and directly. It is true that he now spends a good deal of time away from his mother, playing round the streets and on the rough waste ground which is a natural, and rather dangerous, adventure playground for the local children.

Jimmie does not say much in school to his teachers; he responds to their talk by nods and gestures. He often seems not to heed the teacher's requests and continues to do the things she asks him to stop. Sometimes he listens to her as though puzzled and then looks round at the other children and copies whatever they are doing. One cannot blame the teacher for thinking that Jimmie is unable to use or understand much language. She wonders if perhaps he is deaf but by informal testing finds that this seems not to be the case. So she comes to the conclusion that he is rather dull, though she still remarks about his quickness with tools, and any practical task which is demonstrated to him.

It is when speech is involved that Jimmie fails to respond adequately. The following comes from the record of the teacher's talk in her classroom made during one morning. The record was made with her agreement; she had become interested in the problems language presents to children and learned a great deal from discussing the record of her talk, and those made of other teachers, who formed a study group to consider ways of communicating with young children in school:

Teacher: Would you pick the towel up for me before someone treads on it?

Jimmy looks at the towel, looks round and walks away.

Teacher: What do we do with the towel Jimmie?

Jimmie stares at her—shakes his head a little—turns away.

Teacher: Well, would you like to hang it up?

Jimmie shakes his head slowly, smiles, walks away.

Teacher (*sounds exasperated*): Jimmie, pick the towel up.
Now hang it up.

Jimmie picks up towel, looks round.

Teacher: On the bottom row.

Jimmie looks bewildered, begins to put it on shelf under the seat close to the floor.

Teacher: Oh, come on, Jimmie, listen to me—put it here on the peg.

She points to the peg and Jimmie hangs the towel up, smiles and runs off. Later, Jimmie is in the water tray.

Teacher: Hadn't you better cover your jersey up Jimmie?

Jimmie looks puzzled and looks round.

Teacher (*in kindly tone*): Well, what about it?

Jimmie stands looking up at her, hands stretched out in water.

Teacher: Wouldn't you like an apron on?

Jimmie looks worried, shakes his head. He moves away quickly as the teacher moves towards him, then runs over to where Billy and Tim are playing with blocks. Jimmie stands and watches, then joins in. He is not rebuffed and settles to play. Later:

Teacher: Where are the people who were using the blocks?

No response from Jimmie.

Teacher: The boys who were building? Well?

Child: I think Jimmie was.

Teacher: Jimmie—would you like to tidy them away now Jimmie, before you have your milk?

Jimmie starts to move across the room, the teacher turns away. Jimmie walks to milk table and sits down on a spare chair. He smiles at the other children and picks up a bottle of milk and begins to drink. Teacher notices bricks again.

Teacher: I wonder who has forgotten to clear away?

She speaks loudly and looks around.

Teacher: Someone has forgotten to put his bricks away. I wonder who.

Child: I think it's Jimmie.

Teacher: I remember, Jimmie, yes, I remember—fancy forgetting to do your clearing up. We don't do things like that do we? What will happen if you don't do your own jobs Jimmie?

Jimmie looks very embarrassed and sucks hard on his straw.

Teacher: Now you don't want someone else to do it for you, do you? Well, then —

She waits—but Jimmie keeps on drinking.

Teacher: Jimmie, do you hear me? Come and put your bricks away quickly.

Jimmie finishes his milk, and runs across and begins to throw bricks into the box.

Later: the teacher is now looking at Jimmie's drawing.

Teacher: That's nice Jimmie. What can you tell me about your picture?

Jimmie: —House.

Teacher: Yes, it is a very nice house. Whoever lives in it I wonder.

Jimmie says nothing.

Teacher: Does somebody live in it Jimmie?

Jimmie: It's a house—my house.

Teacher: Do you live in it?

Jimmie shakes his head.

Teacher: Well it's very nice. Do you want to take it home?

Jimmie looks up at her and smiles.

Teacher: Put it in your pocket then.

Jimmie folds up his picture and puts it in his pocket.

The teacher speaks to everybody.

Teacher: Nearly time for Mummies to come. Come round everybody—come along—we'll sing before we go home.

Jimmie follows the example of others, sits down and listens to teacher singing but does not join in.

Jimmie's teacher was surprised to know how little talk Jimmie had been involved in during the morning. She remembered speaking to him but had hardly been aware of his bewilderment, because on each occasion she had moved on very quickly to speak to other children.

From what we have seen of the kind of talk that Jimmie has experienced with his mother it is quite possible that Jimmie was very unsure of what was expected of him. Certainly he was very unaccustomed to the form 'Would you like to —?' or 'Wouldn't you like —?'

The use of this form might suggest that there is choice here, whereas, in fact, in a home like Mark's both mother and child treat this as though it were a firm instruction. Jimmie, however, is quite unaccustomed to this 'oblique' request, and it isn't until he is directed 'Pick up the towel,' or 'Clear up the bricks' that he finds a familiar form of message.

Much of the teacher's management of this class is accomplished by oblique requests, or the appeal 'Whoever has forgotten?' The form of the request suggests that choices are possible: perhaps the teacher does not recognise that the form suggests choice, but her expectations are that these oblique requests will be responded to as though they were directives. Mark would have responded in this way. Jimmie, however, may not be familiar with this form, so that he has not learnt the expected response: in fact he is rarely in communication with his teacher during this recording because he does not share the meaning of her requests.

It is interesting too that all the teacher's talk was concerned with ways of behaving, but couched in a very different form from that of Jimmie's mother. There is very little attempt to talk with Jimmie. The question about his drawing supposed that he was identifying the house he had drawn with someone who lived in it. 'My house' was taken to mean 'The house I live in' not 'My drawing of a house.'

Jimmie's offering of a comment about his picture might have been an indication that here was something that had meaning for him and which offered an opportunity for him to be encouraged to express that meaning in talk.

In the recorded episode we can see that Jimmie often seemed puzzled: he responded to 'Would you like to tidy them (the bricks) away now before you have your milk' by running across to have his milk, as though the only part of the message he had understood was 'have your milk.' Perhaps it was. He responds to the request to hang his towel on the bottom row by trying to push his towel under the seat. Perhaps this was in response to 'bottom' and the notion of 'row' was not one that he understood.

It is difficult for teachers, and adults who have had great experience of using language, and who are able to select words to express fine distinctions in meaning, and who respond appropriately to ambiguity because the context is recognised, to appreciate the problems for the child who has already learnt to look for a different set of cues and who fails to find them. He can only respond to those bits of the teacher's language that stand out as meaningful to him. For the rest, he may assume that because he is not controlled by direct demands that there is no control being exerted by the teacher. At times he appears disobedient, and at times he appears to behave as though he believes that no one minds what he does. He fails to understand his teacher because the ways in which he has learnt to use, and to expect adults to use, language do not serve him usefully in this new situation.

In a situation like this change can only come from the teacher. Clearly Jimmie's home experience is not going to alter, and is going to continue to foster the attitudes and ways of using language that Jimmie had already learnt. Nor does the solution seem to lie in the teacher trying to reproduce the kind of talk that Jimmie is used to: although he might by this means be made to feel more at ease, it is hardly likely to develop attitudes which will help him to use his school experiences more profitably.

Jimmie's teacher decided that she must try to help Jimmie discover what was expected of him in the classroom. She deliberately began to give clearer directions, supporting her own 'Would you?' or 'Will you?' by courteous requests. Thus, for example, after saying 'Perhaps we should begin to clear up now' she was careful to add 'Please stop now, and put the things you are using away', or after 'Could you tidy up the floor Jimmie?' added 'Put the bricks in the box now and the paper in the waste basket.' In this way, perhaps, Jimmie would learn the expected ways of working in this classroom, and know that the limits of behaviour were very clearly set. Perhaps too he would learn the meaning of this form of request which is at first so alien to his experience.

His teacher's expectations about general behaviour and her ways of controlling children is only one of the problems of communication between Jimmie and his teacher. Quite frequently the teacher will ask for explanations or reasons and these also may present Jimmie with an unfamiliar role. The following are some of the questions, recorded during a morning's observation which were put directly to Jimmie or to the group:

1 Why do you want more bricks Jimmie?
2 How do you think the milk got to school?
3 Why does mummy hang the washing on the line?
4 Why do you want a blue crayon?
5 Which way do you want me to cut the paper?
6 What did you do when you went into the shop?

Here the questioner is assuming that the child is not only able to reflect on his experiences and to anticipate his intentions, but also that he will have sufficient command of language to understand the question and frame an answer to it. But if Jimmie's home has not provided much experience of this kind he may be unaccustomed to receiving questions of this kind and so unpractised in answering them.

There are other assumptions that we make about children's

skill and understanding. For example, we may take it for granted that pictures are meaningful to children whatever their experience. Some mothers introduce their children to books and pictures at a very early age, often as early as six months, and from then onwards the child has regular experiences of looking at books with mother or with father. Gradually, from first giving names for the people and objects in the picture, the child learns to structure the scene, relating one part to another; he learns to make sense of what he sees. Moreover, he learns to extract a story from a series of pictures ordered from left to right and to relate what happens in one picture to what has gone before and that which follows. Many children when they come to nursery school have already had much experience of books and of interpreting and talking about pictures. These children expect to be asked to talk about pictures, or will do it without waiting for an invitation: they continue in school to use the skills which have been learned at home.

But this is not necessarily the case with children like Jimmie. His parents may not have seen this as a way of helping the child to interesting experiences: they read little themselves and there are few books in the home. Jimmie's mother said when asked if Jimmie liked to look at books:

He's only started looking at books now he's at school. It's useless to give him them at home. He'd only tear them—well they do, don't they?—I mean, he's not really big enough to know better yet, is he? No we don't look at them at home— we leave it for school—it's enough during the day isn't it?

Talking about a picture or a book may be an activity which is quite new for Jimmie: he has not had years of experience, of learning that it is interesting to look at and talk about books, and that the pictures are to be seen as puzzles to be solved. Before the teacher can expect Jimmie to do more than identify some of the objects in the picture she will need to provide Jimmie with some essential experiences that other children have already had at home, to talk with him, developing new attitudes and helping him to enjoy talking about pictures.

There are other uses of language which will be alien to Jimmie and with which his teacher may assume he is already familiar, but perhaps enough has been said here to indicate the problems that are caused for a child if the teacher assumes that all children have met with the same experiences and developed the same skills. Jimmie's expectations are obviously not in tune with those of his teacher, and only time spent with her can change this. There is little Jimmie can do to help himself; he can only learn these necessary skills from frequent interchange with an adult who is aware of his need for help. The teacher may be the only person who is able to give him the help he needs.

How can the teacher help Jimmie? We shall attempt to answer this question in later chapters but it seems clear that the assumptions that the teacher expressed about Jimmie in a way prevented her looking more closely at his problem. Suppose Jimmie had been a member of Mark's family, then the teacher, expecting Jimmie to be like the rest of the family, would have perhaps said:

> I don't understand this—why is Jimmie not like the rest of his family? I must try to find out what makes him so different so that I can help him.

Because Jimmie fits the expected pattern perhaps she dismisses him as like the rest. Yet Jimmie is a bright little boy, and there is a clue to this if she will be sensitive to it. He sees how to do a job quickly. When working at the bench he looks carefully for a piece of wood that will serve his purpose. He examines several and discards them before he is satisfied and then we can see that it is just the right size for the tail of the aeroplane he is making: it is in proportion to the rest. Jimmie often keeps an eye on his neighbour, waiting to see what he does, and then, taking the lead from him, he has accomplished the task more quickly than his model. This is not the behaviour of a dull four-year-old. When it was pointed out to the teacher she knew that she really had already observed this, but her preconceived picture of Jimmie had not allowed her to admit it as evidence.

Obviously, the teacher has a difficult task: there are just too many children for her to see them as individuals all the time. But it is the case that some children may be written off by their teachers, almost before they start school because of the expectations the teacher has already formed.

When children come to school, whether at the age of three or four or five, they come with well established attitudes towards people, and with an orientation and expectancy about ways of using language. The persistent exposure to particular uses of language as part of the way of life in his home, has already built within the child a disposition to go on using language in this same way. Moreover, the habitual uses of language in the home reflect and transmit particular ways of organising meaning. So we must realise too that the differences between children in the way in which they use language may reflect differences at a deeper level: the differences may lie in the set of meanings which they hold, and to which each child must refer in his attempts to deal with new experiences.

We have perhaps said enough to show that for some children coming to school will not be only a matter of entering a strange physical and social environment, but also of meeting unaccustomed ways of using language. For some children what has been learnt in the home will be excellent preparation for life in school, and for talking with the teacher; for other children, however, the ways of talking which have been learnt in the home may prove to be seriously inadequate for dealing with new experiences, for interpreting teachers' talk and for responding in ways expected by teachers.

Chapter 5

Listening to Children's Talk

Mothers, and those who work with young children, recognise, as they listen to the young child talking, that he makes advances in the use of language almost daily. He may say something new, master the articulation of a sound which before has eluded him, demonstrate an awareness of another grammatical rule, add to his vocabulary, or show increased understanding of what is said to him. We delight in his new achievement, and so his further efforts are encouraged. For the most part, however, this recognition of progress is quite intuitive, for there are such wide differences in the way in which children learn to use language between the ages of one year and four, that it is difficult to discover whether there is some pattern that all will follow, or to decide what a child could be expected to have learned by any particular age. Some children will be talking almost like adults before the age of three, whilst others will, by comparison, be much later in gaining such facility; yet by five they may both be using language with great skill. The child's readiness to talk, however, may disguise the fact that the uses he puts it to are limited.

If we are to help children to develop a range of uses of language we need, first of all, to be able to make some appraisal of the child's skill in using language. Is it possible for the teacher who has some knowledge of how to approach the task, to guide each child through a range of different uses of language, developing in each a sensitivity to the appropriateness of his language for the particular purpose he pursues? This suggests that we should not only be aware of the child's skill in using language, but that we must know also about the most profitable ways of talking with him.

The teacher will, therefore, need to become either an eavesdropper, or an attentive audience before the kind of help needed by the child can be understood or given. With twenty or thirty children in the group, this may be a formidable task. The teacher, however, generally spends much time talking to children and very much less in listening to their talk; smaller classes would make the task easier, but would not necessarily ensure that the teacher would help the child more effectively. To do this the needs of the child must be appraised and that means, first of all, listening carefully to what the child says.

We know that all teachers should listen to children—but do we often do this? Let us for a moment look at Mrs P as she works with her three- to-five-year-olds. The room and adjoining terrace are invitingly laid out before school begins. As those who arrive early come in, there is a smile and a word of greeting:

Hello John, how are you today? Come and give me a hand with the slide, will you? It's going to be a lovely day I think so we'll put the slide on the terrace, shall we? Oh, and there's Mary, hello Mary dear, what a pretty ribbon you have in your hair today, haven't you? Did mummy put it in? Will you fill the water jars for the painting please? And put the paint tins on the tables will you? Can you do that? And here's Peter—I like your flowers—oh, are they for me? How lovely! Thank you very much—that is kind of you. Will you find a jug in the cupboard? I'm sure you would like to put them in. Would you like someone to help you? Yes, Mary, if you've finished you can help Peter. You'd like that wouldn't you Peter? Yes, I knew you would.

Mrs P exudes friendliness, warmth and acceptance. The children are comfortable with her and smile and nod eagerly, pleased at the welcome they receive. Mrs P anticipates each child's response to the activities which are being provided for him, most of which he is already familiar with. This is Mrs P's style. The children are happy and secure, and there is plenty to occupy them. There are few disruptions to this 'get busy and enjoy yourself' atmosphere.

Susie comes in—her face is tearful as a bigger sister nudges her over to Mrs P. Mrs P turns and immediately falls to her knees, drawing Susie towards her.

> Don't cry Susie—there's a dear! Wait a minute—let me dry your eyes—there, there, what happened? Did Angie push you (shake of head)—no? What was it then? Did you hurt yourself? (shake of head)—what then? You lost something?

And so the teacher's language flows.

Mrs P is so anxious that her children shall feel welcome and secure that she devotes all her talking to this end. Language envelops the child—but he rarely needs, or is given, an opportunity to respond except with 'Yes' or 'No' for Mrs P rarely stops to listen.

Her assistant, Miss S, a nursery nurse, has a rather different style. She is young and has just completed her training. Her manner is light and bantering.

> Well, Billy boy, and what have you to say for yourself today? Come on, David, you can't use all the sand—now can you?—let Alan have some too. Now, now, Tarzan—watch where you go. Oh, Lucy—not *all* the flour dear—leave some for the next people.

Miss S looks delightful, trim and crisp. Her speech is kindly, and she gives clear directions. She manages the children with a pleasant, easy manner and tears are rare. She anticipates problems and by pleasant directives, disguised by the light teasing tone, manages to avoid clashes between children, or between herself and the children.

Altogether this is a happy satisfying place to be in, and it can be seen from the following recorded comments how the children are encouraged to take part in many activities.

> Mrs P: Let me see Paul—you'll need something to stick that with—I'll help you—here's the sellotape—there—good.
>
> Miss S: The sand isn't very good for pies today, is it?

Wait a minute I'll put some water in—mix it up and make it nice—now try that.

Mrs P: It would be nice to have a party! Put your aprons on—we'll make some cakes.

The children are carried along by Mrs P and Miss S. They are immersed in the teacher's language, but there is little invitation or even apparent need for the children to talk to the adults. It's almost as though anything they might say has been anticipated, and for the teachers it is much quicker than waiting for the child to speak, especially when she feels that she knows exactly what the child wants and what he would say if only she had time to wait. And there are so many children to keep busy!

If we listened to the way in which language is used in Mrs P's and Miss S's group, we would see that although they are creating a warm atmosphere in which children are secure, happy, encouraged to venture in making and doing, experiencing success and praise, they are neglecting to use the situations, which they have made such efforts to provide, for the promotion of the children's intellectual development. Mrs P and Miss S do not seem to expect the children to think at all and because of this, perhaps, they fail to seize the opportunities, which they themselves have made possible, for helping the children to develop their skills in using language through their efforts to communicate with the adults.

But is this so important? After all, these two adults, in providing so much to do, and maintaining the flow of play and goodwill between children, do provide conditions in which these twenty-five children have time to talk and much to talk about amongst themselves. Since the group contains threes, fours and fives at different stages of maturity, it would seem that there must be ample opportunity for children to learn from one another. Perhaps in this kind of regime the teacher needs only to be aware of the oldest, most able children, and to talk with them, because the rest can surely learn from each other.

This argument is one which is often advanced by parents, students and teachers, and to a certain extent it is true. A doctor will often recommend that a child who is slow to begin to speak should go to a nursery, and here he may quickly begin to do his share of talking. This seems to happen because the child is provoked into using language more: he must begin to be more energetic in his use of speech just because he becomes involved in activities in which he wants to play a part—a part which demands language as an aid to his own success.

How much do children learn from one another? In this episode Jane, aged five, plays in the house corner and talks with Pattie who is two and a half.

Jane: There, Pattie, put your baby to bed.
Pattie: Baby to bed. Go sleep baby.
Jane: Now us mummies will make the dinner, won't we?
Pattie: Make dinner now. Me make dinner.
Jane: Get a pan then—here you are. I'm going to make a pudding.
Pattie: Me make pudding.
Jane: No—no—we don't want two puddings. You make something else.
Pattie: Make tea.
Jane: No—it's dinner-time not tea-time—you'll have to do the 'tatoes.
Pattie: Not 'tatoes. Not want 'tatoes me.
Jane: You'll have to. You have to have 'tatoes for dinner.

The listening teacher might have recognised this situation as pregnant with possibilities both for encouraging thinking and for a more profitable use of language for Pattie.

The discussion of what kind of food is generally associated with lunch-time or tea-time might have been taken up, or the reasons why two puddings would be too much of a good thing. A discussion might have been developed of the kind of utensils to be used for making dinner, or the kind of heat source to be used, or the kind of dishes the child would like for dinner: choosing a menu might have motivated the young child to recall her own preferences.

Or again, the listening teacher might have recognised the need to remodel some of the two-year-old's utterances, for example:

Pattie: Baby to bed. Go sleep baby.
Adult: Your baby is going to bed is she?
Does she want to go to sleep now?

Or:

Pattie: Me make dinner.
Adult: You're going to make the dinner Pattie.
What are you going to make?

We can see that Jane is using Pattie as a useful addition to her own play but she is not likely to modify her talk so that the younger child may understand. Nor is she likely to correct her own errors so that the younger child may have a good example to follow. Nor is she interested, as the adult would be, in helping the younger child to see the logicality of arguments, to relate the cause with its effect. The older child is not likely to stop and be interested in what the younger child is saying because of an interest in the younger child's intellectual prowess or because the younger child has some misunderstanding.

If we rely on children learning from one another it may restrict their learning in many ways. We are not saying that children do not learn or benefit from talking with other children. The point we would make here is that young children cannot deliberately choose the language they use, the responses they make, with another child's need in mind. They make their choices because of the meaning inherent in the situation for themselves: they may or may not facilitate the other child's thinking and expression of ideas. The teacher who is listening and who is alert and knowledgeable about ways of using language, on the other hand, may by a single comment influence the direction of the child's talk, or help him to pursue an idea which might otherwise have been only partially explored.

It is important, then to listen to a child's talk so that we might judge how we might help him. It follows therefore, that we must put him into a situation in which he is ready and able to talk. This means first and foremost, that the atmosphere of the nursery must be one which encourages the child to talk easily with children and with adults.

If, however, the teacher has little knowledge of understanding of the part played by language in the child's learning, or feels that the important thing about speech is to have the child speaking correctly and politely, a great deal of effort may be put into correcting the child, which is likely to have quite the opposite effect of the one intended, as does Miss H in the example quoted below, which is typical of her efforts to improve the child's use of speech:

Tommy: Can I have the scissors?
Miss H: May I have the scissors, *please*, Miss H?
Try again Tommy.
Tommy: I want some scissors.
Miss H: Well then you must say 'May I have the scissors please Miss H?'
Let me hear you say that.
Tommy: Can I —
Miss H: May I—now.
Tommy: May I—can I have the scissors?
Miss H: Oh, Tommy, say—please.
Tommy: Please—the scissors.

Later:

Tommy: My mam gave me a penny and I —
Miss H: Gave, Tommy, not gived.
Start again—my mum gave me a penny—say that.
Tommy: My mum—she gived
Miss H: Tommy—gave —
Tommy: She gaved me a penny and —
Miss H: She *gave* you a penny did she? All right—you *are* lucky—run along now.

Tommy's efforts at engaging his teacher in conversation, and giving her important information, are hardly ever successful. It is fortunate that he is persistent, except that even with his persistence he rarely manages to succeed in getting the teacher to listen to what he wants to tell her.

We might expect that children who are less persistent than Tommy will give up the struggle and learn to keep quiet when the teacher is near if all their experiences of talk are of this kind.

We are not saying that Tommy should not learn the grammatical and social conventions, but only that this is a very unproductive way of setting about it and that offering opportunities for the expression of information through talk, which, when taken, will be rewarded by the adult's interest and response to that information, is far more important at this stage.

Mrs R tackles a similar situation in quite a different way. She has been watching and listening to Billy as he builds with boxes. Billy is a robust, perky, four-and-a-half-year old, and John, a rather timid child nearing five. Mrs R chooses a moment of tension at which to intervene in the children's talk:

John has bumped into the bus Billy made from boxes.

Billy: Get out of the way—go on get away—it's my bus.

Billy threatens John by standing up and pushing him away. John's face reddens and he looks upset.

Mrs R: Hello, Billy, doesn't John want to ride on your bus?
Billy: He pushed it.
John: I didn't push it—I didn't.
Mrs R: I expect John wants to be your passenger—do you John?
John: No—I want to get in it.
Mrs R: That's what a passenger does—he gets in and rides in the bus. I wonder what the bus driver says to the passenger—Billy?
Billy: Tickets, tickets—like that.

Billy laughs.

Mrs R: Yes he does—he says 'Tickets please, have your money ready please.'
Billy: He's got a bag and a ticket thing hasn't he?
John: And he says 'Hold tight please!'
Mrs R: Does the bus driver always say please?
John: Yes—yes—he does, and my mam says 'Next stop please.'
Mrs R: Why do people say 'please' when they ask other people to do things I wonder?

Billy: So they'll do it—what they want—they'll do it.
Mrs R :   Is that what you think John?
John: My mam says—'say please' then she gives me all things.

John laughs.

Mrs R :   What's this bus driver going to say to the passenger now?
Billy: Sit down *please*—money *please*—like that.
John: My mam says—says—want to get off please.
Mrs R :   Yes—that's what the passengers say isn't it—what your mum says when she's a passenger. Now driver, will you stop the bus please, I must get off here.

Billy and John laugh and make a loud sound of braking.

Mrs R seems to have found a much more useful way of helping her children to understand why they are expected to be courteous to other people. She is helping the children to understand that it is a good thing to adopt this form of request. She helps them to put themselves in the position of other people, and to practise the use of 'please' as they try out the other person's role. The children are invited to draw on their memories of travelling in buses and of adults using 'please' with each other. John brings the discussion home, to himself—'My mam says —' Mrs R not only helps Billy and John to accept the 'please' formula but also manages to stimulate them to think and to express their ideas through talk.

Similarly in helping children to correct their mistakes, to recognise a grammatical regularity or irregularity, Mrs R listens closely and then chooses a moment when the correction will not stem the flow of talk but will stimulate another kind of discussion.

Of course, it may not always be appropriate to press the child to talk at all. Some shy children or children overwhelmed by any suggestion of criticism would perhaps be under great strain if so much were demanded of them, for questioning and discussing in this way focuses the attention of the teacher and of others who are near, on the child or children who might be expected to answer. Only the teacher's knowledge of the child, gained from observation, from listening, and perhaps from talking with the child's mother and other teachers, can inform the teacher about the problems of the oversensitive child. Such children need the same kind of consideration that is shown to very new children, for in their case, the tactful handling must continue longer, since they require so much reassurance before they are at ease with other people.

The new child particularly, needs a sympathetic listener to his problems and complaints and what the teacher says and the way in which she says it will be most important. The teacher will need to be reassuring, soothing, cheerful and calm, talking to the child about his family, and particularly about his mother, his brothers and sisters, and his home. The teacher's talk aims at helping the child to understand that home is there waiting for his return. This is the time when the teacher will talk without expecting to get any spoken response from the child. When the child finally responds with speech, hesitantly at first perhaps, the teacher will react warmly, encouraging relaxation and acceptance, or dispelling fears and doubts. As the child relaxes and begins to move more confidently about the nursery, the teacher's talk will be used to draw the child gradually into the pattern and expectancies of the nursery. Once the child begins to talk readily the teacher can learn much about his ability to use language by listening to him whenever she can.

Chapter 6

Observing Children's Use of Language

We have emphasised the importance of the teacher listening to the child talking in order to gain information about his use of language. What is it that the teacher will listen for?

Perhaps the first thing we need to know about the child as he adjusts to his life in school is how readily he uses speech with adults and other children. This might be discovered by observing the child from time to time during the day and watching his activity. Particular attention would be paid to what he said when he approached the teacher and how he responded when the teacher approached him and engaged him in conversation. Can everything the child says be distinguished without too much effort? If not, what is it that makes it difficult to understand what the child says? Is it that he speaks too quickly or too slowly, that his intonation is unusual, or that he has problems of articulation? If so, which particular sounds does he have difficulty in producing? This question may not be easy to answer if the difficulty is so great that the teacher cannot distinguish the words he uses at all. In this case looking at a book and asking the child to name objects and people in the pictures will help the teacher to track down the several sounds which the child finds difficult to articulate.

The child who is not able to speak clearly enough to be understood by his listener may be extremely frustrated and unhappy and may become aggressive because he is not understood, or withdraw into himself, avoiding contact with others so that he may not be embarrassed by his failure to speak clearly. The teacher will judge, from knowledge about the child and the extent of his difficulty, whether the problem should be discussed with the mother, and whether she should be advised to consult a doctor, psychologist, or speech therapist.

Usually, however, the difficulties are minor ones and probably do not hinder communication. Once the sounds the child has difficulty with have been identified by the teacher he can be helped best by unobtrusive methods. The teacher can devise games or jingles which can be taken with the small group with which the child is playing, in an informal spontaneous way and for fun. The inability to roll the 'r' is a common one, but one which, once it is recognised by the listener, does not impede intelligibility. The child can be encouraged whilst playing with motor cars or by pretending to be a motor car himself to practise the rolled 'r'. The problem is how to help the child with his difficulty without making him self-conscious about it; but leaving the problem and hoping it will be outgrown may not be in the best interests of the child.

As she listens to a child's talk the teacher will be also noting other characteristics of the child's speech. She will want to discover whether he uses only one or two word utterances in the manner of a two-year-old, or whether he relies mainly on gesture, tapping the teacher's leg, or pulling at her skirt for attention.

The teacher may note that the child makes quite long utterances but that he has many babyisms still, or that he still uses his own name, or 'me' instead of the pronoun I. Often the best way to help a child here is to invite him to identify with a puppet, doll, or animal and to pretend to speak for it, using 'I want —,' or 'I have —.' or 'I see —.' or 'I like —' as a natural part of the play. Sometimes the teacher will speak for puppets or dolls or animals and this allows the point to be made naturally.

By paying special attention to one child's talking for a few minutes on several occasions the teacher can learn about the child's difficulties and can then hold them in mind and find ways of helping him as opportunities arise naturally during the day.

The teacher can as she observes the child, note the kind and frequency of the contacts he makes with other people, and the occasions on which she sees him speak to another child or to another adult.

The duration of the contact can be observed, whether there are several exchanges in the conversation, or whether it is a short question and answer contact. Does the child use his speech to threaten or criticise his playmates, or does he seem to use language to 'get on' with the children he plays with? Does the child seem to take the lead in the group and use his speech to establish his leadership, issuing instructions to the other? Is he a follower, or a complainer, or does he stand and watch without saying anything?

From short but frequent viewing of the child during the day it is possible for the teacher to build up a picture of how readily and for what purposes the child seems to be using language. When it seems suitable the teacher can settle where she can listen more closely to what the child is saying for a few minutes so that she may make some appraisal of the purposes for which he uses language and of the kind of skill he displays.

We would expect to hear the child using language as a means of gaining a feeling of success or superiority, and to maintain his own comfort and pleasure and status, and to fend off any trespass on his person, property and rights.

Some observation can be made of the general character of this language: is it almost always aggressive, abusive or demanding, or has the child learned to use more acceptable ways of communicating his needs so that he only rarely resorts to expressing himself aggressively? If he has, then this suggests that he is selecting his language with an awareness of the way in which the listener might be expected to respond. The child who approaches the one who has taken one of his personal possessions and says 'I'd like my car now because I want to play with it' rather than demanding it with 'Give me that car, it's mine' shows that he seeks to justify his claim to the other. In other words he recognises the need to give explanations justifying his actions.

The young child also uses much of his talk for making a running commentary on what is happening in the world around him. Thus he reports:

'There's a fish in the tank and it's swimming around'—or:
'We've got blue and yellow paint today'—or:
'The sand is not wet'—or:
'That's a big piece.'

It is as though the child is monitoring his experience and trying to organise it at a simple level.

But the child may set his ongoing experience against a frame of reference built from past experience within which he seeks to derive additional meaning for each new experience. Thus he might say:

The fish swimming in there is not like the one I have at home, it's different because mine has stripes on it, but this one hasn't. And mine's bigger than this.'

By recalling information from other experiences this child sees his present experience of fish not as an isolated incident, but as part of continuing and extending knowledge about fish. He compares two experiences seeking for the distinguishing features.

We would also expect to find that every child uses a good deal of language to accompany his actions, almost as though keeping himself in touch with his own actions and activities:

I'm putting this dolly into bed.
Covering her up now.
Push the bed over here—like that.
Looking for a book now.

Much of this monitoring language would seem to be addressed to no one in particular; the child may seem to be talking to himself or for himself. This is very common behaviour in children of nursery school age.

Again, the child may use language at a more complex level of involvement with his and other people's actions. He may use language to concentrate his attention on a particular task, or to initiate action, or control the actions of other people. Often such uses of language can be seen as assisting and directing collaboration, justifying or explaining happenings as they occur, as in the following examples:

1 You put your brick on top and I'll hold the tower so it won't fall down.
2 Mind your car out of the way so mine won't crash with it.

3 Put that ladder here—I'll hold it so you can climb up.

4 If you don't push hard we can't open it.

The child will not only use language to obtain collaboration but very often in doing this he will extend his play activity. Such instances may provide evidence that the child is capable of using language to achieve a particular objective.

All children also seem to use language for the creation of imaginary situations for their play. The child injects new meaning into the present concrete situation representing new features which can only exist for others if a statement about the imagined situation is made through language.

The child may take some bricks and announce that they are a road, or put on a hat and announce that he is a queen or a policeman. All children seem likely to use language for this purpose, if only at the level of announcing 'I'm a soldier' or 'I'm a baddy.' It would be the absence of this kind of behaviour that should be noted for this might indicate that the child needs help to play and make representation of this kind.

All children, however, may not use language to extend the imaginary situation beyond the labelling of materials and people. Much imaginative play, however, depends for its existence, for the participants as well as the spectators, on the representation through language of ideas, as in the following examples:

1 And pretend you're a robber and you're sticking up a train.

2 And jump into the water—swim like me.

3 You be the doctor and I'm the poorly baby.

This kind of activity would seem to be important in that it depends for its existence on the conjuring up from earlier experiences, which may have been secondhand or vicarious experiences, a new experience which does not exist in the reality of the actual and present world, but only in the activities of the child's inner world and his symbolic use of materials.

It would seem important to look for evidence that the child is able to use language in this way. Play of this kind provides its own motivation for reflecting knowledge about other people, and for trying to feel and act as they do.

There are other uses to which language can be put which seem to be important for promoting and expressing thinking of various kinds: these may be summed up as analysing, anticipating and predicting and would be the basis of such activities as planning, and problem solving. The teacher will be alert to note any instances of any of these more complex uses of language. They will be less frequent than others and therefore may be distinguished more easily and noted.

Clearly the teacher is often in a dilemma when deciding how time with children might best be spent: is it more important to spend a few minutes listening to a child to note his disposition and skill in using language, or should she deliberately press him to talk for a particular purpose? We shall discuss ways of talking in order to encourage particular uses of language in a later chapter, but what is clear is that unless the teacher listens to the child and gains some picture of the ways in which he uses language, deliberate efforts may not, in fact, help the child to gain anything. Indeed the teacher needs to listen first before a profitable move can be made. If the picture gained is of a timid, withdrawn child who is afraid to make contacts, then the teacher will not be worrying about how to stimulate the child to use language more, but rather, attention will be centred on helping the child to find a friend and to make a good relationship with one or more of the adults. Until this is accomplished, and the child feels secure enough to use speech freely it will not be possible to gain a true picture of the child's ability.

Chapter 7

The Invitation to Talk

If the child's development of language is to be promoted when he comes to school then clearly the teacher must be able to judge what it is that should be done to help him. The first objective must be to develop a relationship with the child in which he will talk readily. Only when he reveals the way in which he is able to use language is it possible to observe the kind of uses to which he puts his language and to note the kind of difficulties that he has.

The way in which the teacher responds to the child's talk will be crucial in determining whether he will continue his efforts or not. If the teacher shows that she is a willing listener, and has time to give to listening to him, communicated to the child perhaps because she sits down beside him, giving him undivided attention for a short time, then his confidence in his own ability to talk with her is likely to grow.

One of the most useful ways of encouraging the child to go on talking is just to nod the head, smile, and indicate continuing interest by saying 'mm?' or 'yes' or 'really!' or similar comments which really communicate to the child 'Go on—I'm listening with great interest.' The following example shows how a range of such 'I'm still listening' devices sustained Richard's talk. He hesitantly initiated the conversation as he picked up a snowstorm novelty that had been placed on one of the side tables by the teacher, who thought it would create interest and opportunities for talking.

Richard:	See this thing.
Mrs O:	Mm.
Richard:	Well, I've got one like it.
Mrs O:	Really.

Richard: Well, it isn't like it really.

Mrs O: No?

Richard: It's just a house—my one.

Mrs O: Mm?

Richard: But when you shake it—well—it's like this—see it snows.

Mrs O nods and smiles.

Mrs O: Yes, I see.

Richard: But mine's broke now.

Mrs O: Oh dear.

Richard: Yes, it's broke.

Mrs O: Mm?

Richard: On the fireplace—my dad's fireplace.

Mrs O: Mm?

Richard: I was running and I fell—that's how it broke.

Mrs O: I see.

Richard: Yes—and we've got a new fireplace now.

Mrs O: Have you?

Richard: It's a red one—and—it's in my dad's garage—the broken one is.

Mrs O: I see.

Richard: And my dad—it cost a lot of money.

Richard was not very confident about talking and direct questioning did not seem to help him. But on this occasion Mrs O was giving him her undivided attention, and her quiet exclamations and listening attitude seemed to give Richard just enough support and encouragement to go on and say more. If the teacher can wait, restraining herself from asking questions or saying much herself, the child will often say a good deal which is unprompted. If the waiting time extends so that it seems the child will not continue, then a repetition of his last remark may assure him of the teacher's continued listening and interest and encourage him to say more.

Michele is diffident about talking with adults and needs encouragement to maintain a conversation for more than one or two utterances, as we see in the next example.

Michele: And my mum's poorly.
Miss T: Oh dear—I *am* sorry.
Michele: She falled—and—and —

The pause lengthens.

Miss T: Your mum fell over, did she?
Michele: Yes—yes—she did, she fell over—over our Lassie
          you see.

Miss T nods and waits—but the pause lengthens and Michele
seems to be withdrawing interest.

Miss T: Your mum fell over Lassie?
Michele: Yes—that's our dog—Lassie.
          She fell over her—and she hurted her leg.
Miss T: Oh dear—is it very bad?
Michele: Yes—she's in a chair—she can't walk.

Michele shakes her head and becomes thoughtful. Miss T
waits for a while.

Miss T: You say she can't walk.
Michele: No—she can't—'cos it hurts—she just sits.
Miss T: Mm?
Michele: And my dad—my dad shouted at her.
Miss T: He shouted, did he?
Michele: Yes—he was cross with our Lassie.
Miss T: I expect he *was* cross.

Michele shakes her head.

Michele: Lassie didn't mean to—not to hurt my mum. She
          didn't.

Here we can see that reflecting the child's own comments
encourages her to add more. In the above instance Michele was
being helped to retrieve information from her memory about her
home and parents. The teacher's repetition not only reminded
her of her audience but perhaps helped her to concentrate and
recall another detail. The encouraging but not demanding
reception of her story perhaps encouraged her to find and express
a new meaning for the incidents.

The two episodes quoted here are instances of children making an approach to the teacher. When this happens the teacher has the choice of replying to the child with a question or comment which initiates reference to new aspects that were not in the mind of the child when the approach was made, or of maintaining the child's intention to communicate ideas that were already forming. At first it would seem to be more useful to the child's development of confidence in his own ability to communicate, to choose a strategy which encourages him to pursue and express his own thinking. When the teacher decides that the child needs help if he is to extend his thinking and that a more positive contribution to the conversation would perhaps promote further effort by the child then a choice has to be made, both about the bit of 'meaning' to pursue, and the framing of the question or comment.

In the above example the most profitable approach seems likely to be the one that was adopted, for it encouraged Michele to sustain her own ideas. At the point at which there seemed to be a natural conclusion—'Lassie didn't mean to hurt her'—which was followed by a long pause which the child seemed content to allow to continue, one might judge that the sequence of meaning in the child's mind had been fully expressed. The teacher's question at that point produced the following extension to the conversation:

Michele: Lassie didn't mean to—not to hurt my mum. She didn't.

Miss T: What makes you think that?

Michele: She just sitted down—she didn't do now't.

Miss T: Is Lassie always a good dog?

Michele: No—no—not when she makes a mess.
And she fights—sometimes she does.

Miss T: I wonder what she fights about?

Michele: About—about with a right nasty dog—int' street.

Miss T: What happens then?

Michele: My dad shouts—he goes and shouts and tells it to go away.
And one day—last day— I seed a right big dog—big as that.

Miss T: Was it bigger than Lassie?
Michele: Our Lassie's right little—not as little as Peter's—
that's only so big.

The strategy used by the teacher here is an interesting one. There is not an assault of direct questions; several of the teacher's rejoinders are in the form of an invitation to the child to follow her own meanings. 'What makes you think that?' resulted in Michele looking for some evidence to support her statement. 'I wonder what she fights about?' brought a further comment although not a full explanation. 'What happens then'? is also an open invitation to Michele to follow through the thought about the fighting.

We can see that the course, or strategies, that the teacher adopts will tend to influence the direction and length of the child's contribution. Questions that invite 'yes' or 'no' or a one-word answer are very restricting, as can be seen in the following example.

Mrs W: Are you going to play in the Wendy House, Joanne?
Joanne: Yes.
Mrs W: Can you see the flowers that Jane brought?
Joanne: Yes.
Mrs W: Can you find the dollies?
Joanne: Yes.
Mrs W: Good. Shall you be the mother?
Joanne: Yes—I'm the mother.
Mrs W: What's this?
Joanne: A dress.
Mrs W: And this?
Joanne: A coat.
Mrs W: And this?
Joanne: A hat.
Mrs W: Yes, they're for your dolly. Can you put them on?
Joanne: Yes.

Here we can see that the opportunity to have a few minutes' discussion with Joanne was used to produce a very low level of participation by the child. Joanne was quite at ease although she did not talk very readily, but the strategy used by the teacher here did not seem to be helping the child to reflect on her own experiences and talk about them. The questions were restricting her to following the teacher's comment and to indicating only that she had understood.

The strategy used by the teacher will in the first place be advised by her knowledge of the child and will take into consideration the level of the child's confidence in talking. At first all the teacher's efforts will be directed towards establishing a relationship in which the child is ready and eager to talk and so the teacher's first approach will need to build up a feeling that the child matters, is important as a person, to the teacher. This is, perhaps, done best through the response the teacher gives to the child's approach to her. If immediate interest and appreciation is shown then the child is likely to stay and talk, or at least will make further approaches. If the child cannot make the first approach then the teacher must offer frequent invitations to talk which in themselves imply appreciation of the child's activity without pressing him too hard to reply.

Questions can be oblique, suggesting that a refusal to talk is quite acceptable:

'Do you want to tell me how you made your castle?'—or:
'Can you tell me what you're going to do next?'—or:
'I'm not sure where this ladder should go. Can you tell me what I might do with it?'

In this way, the teacher is able to make a tentative approach to a child which does not seem to demand a reply from those who are still not quite confident about speaking, but at the same time suggests that the teacher recognises their competence to reply as soon as they feel able. It may be that the form of such comments is not fully understood by many young children, but the teacher's tone of voice and intonation, as well as the facial expression, as such forms are used are likely to convey encouragement and tolerance of the child's problems.

But once the child is talking readily, such strategies are still very useful when the matter to be discussed might be judged by the teacher to be in some way rather delicate and the teacher is not sure whether the child will feel able to talk about the matter at all because of his emotional involvement.

We are well aware, however, that for some children such tentativeness and lack of directness might be too ambiguous and therefore generally confusing because this way of talking is not a part of their usual experiences. This may be particularly true of children whose parents never use such tentativeness in their talk, and who expect the adult to demand and give instructions about the behaviour they require.

Once a 'ready-to-talk' attitude on the part of the child has been established then more direct strategies may be appropriate, but questions which place close restriction on possible answers are not likely to help the child to develop an attitude to search for relevant information to give in his response.

Once children are talking readily then strategies which provide a direct challenge will often be judged the most appropriate way of extending the child's use of language. Approaches like 'Tell me why . . . ,' 'Tell me how . . . ,' 'Tell me about . . . ,' or in the question form 'How?,' 'How did you . . .?' 'Why?' 'Why did you . . .?' or 'When are you going to . . .?' or 'What can you tell me about . . .?' or 'What do you think about . . .?' these approaches ask the child to think, to reflect upon something which he has experienced.

Very often there will be confusion, ambiguity, insufficient information for the child to be successful in communicating his intentions to others but he can be helped to make good his failure in communicating by comments such as 'I'm not sure what you mean, will you tell me again?' Sometimes it would seem helpful for the teacher to indicate misunderstanding and to look for the child to correct her as in the example:

Tony: I don't know what to do 'cos they're all too big.
Miss L: You mean the cars are too big?
Tony: No—no—the bricks—they're all too big—I need a little one.

Sometimes the child can be helped to see the listener's problem if the inadequacy of information expressed is made apparent:

Jimmie: Give me that thing there now.
Miss L: Do you mean the scissors?
Jimmie: No—no. Not the scissors. I wanted them wooden
—er—them long things—them wood long pieces.
I'm going to make a road with them.

But perhaps we should help the child more if our questions were set in the kind of conversation we would perhaps hold with our friends. In such a conversation one does not always pose questions but quite frequently makes a comment, offers an explanation, narrates an episode or reveals how one feels about a particular person or situation. In a conversation there is an exchange of information: children need to learn both to receive and to draw information from the people with whom they talk.

If the child can be led to feel that an invitation to talk with his teacher is always open, and that both of them will enjoy what he he has to say, then he is likely to begin to approach her. When the child begins to offer invitations to talk to the teacher then we know that a good relationship is being established.

Chapter 8

Talking to Think

We have emphasised the importance of listening carefully to what children have to say, and giving the child confidence to talk to and with his teachers. Teachers, however, often feel that there is too much talk which goes on at the level of inconsequential chatter and that although such talk may ease relationships between children and between children and their teachers, it certainly does not guarantee that anything of deeper and more lasting value will be accomplished. Perhaps for talk to be valuable we should help the child to pause and think more deeply.

Whilst we would agree that helping the child to think is important, we would not agree that the child learns nothing that is of importance from such conversation. There are several skills that the child needs to discover about how to conduct conversation. Many children, for example, have difficulty in finding an appropriate greeting or an initiating remark, or find it difficult to accept the turn and turn about nature of conversation and are impatient of the delay in completing a sequence of ideas that necessarily must follow when the other person is acknowledging or commenting or reformulating the information or ideas which are emerging.

Ways of asking for different kinds of information must also be learnt, and learning to answer different kinds of questions is clearly important. One important thing that is learnt from conversations is that other people have a point of view that may not be quite the same as one's own: appreciating this, and that other people have feelings and react towards what is said to them with evidence of this, makes the child, as he speaks, begin to consider the other person, so that he is learning to speak for the other rather than speaking only for himself. Many children give short incomplete utterances—incomplete in the sense that the information given is too little for the listener's needs. Until they are able to take into account the listener's needs they cannot be very successful in their attempts to communicate. We can see evidence of this growing skill as a child adds, as it were, afterthought to his first statement and as he shows that he is aware of the need to indicate in a final remark that he intends to close a conversation.

So conversation which may not seem to be demanding much in the way of thinking, may nevertheless be providing essential experiences for some children. Many children by the age of three and four will have already learnt much of this, but other children whose home experiences have not built up within them expectations of this kind, may be quite unskilled in carrying on a conversation. Helping such children into the conventions of holding a conversation is the first step to helping them to use talk for thinking.

How can the teacher help the child to develop an inclination to examine and analyse and make a meaningful structure of his experiences? How can the teacher, through engaging the child in conversation help him to think more deeply?

First of all perhaps the child needs to be made alert to different aspects of his experience. Some children seem to reflect very little of the detail of their experience in their talk, and helping them to build an awareness of aspects they have perhaps learned to ignore is not easy. Useful devices here will be anything that helps the child to be explicit because it is clear that the listener cannot see what the child sees. A kaleidoscope, a peep show, a three dimensional viewer, a 'feely' bag filled with interesting objects makes clear to the child that the listener has not his view. 'Tell me about this' or 'What's happening here?' may help the child to examine the detail carefully. These are the kind of experiences a child will enjoy having time and time again so that it may be possible to help him to move from a description which is essentially one of labelling, to one which appreciates the relationships which exist within the whole.

For example, Gary said on the first occasion when he looked at a peep show which showed a family in a kitchen:

Look—there's a boy and a girl and a lady and a mister.

Questioned 'What else can you tell me about it?' he answered
'There's a cat.'

On that occasion the teacher followed up this response by
talking about the scene with him:

Miss B: Can you see what the people are doing?
Gary: Well the little girl's washing something.
Miss B: Is she? What might she be washing do you think?
Gary: Something dirty.
Miss B: What about the others—can you tell what they're
         doing?
Gary: Yes—well dad's reading his newspaper and that
         boy's playing with the cat.
Miss B: And mother looks as though she's talking to them.
         I wonder what she's saying?
Gary: I don't know.
Miss B: Perhaps she's saying it's time to go to school.
Gary: She is.

A few days later as he looked at the same peep show Gary
structured the scene without help.

Gary: And there's this man, look, reading the paper. And
         those two are going to school—he's playing with the
         cat now. And the girl's washing up for her mum
         before she goes. They've just had their dinner,
         haven't they?

One way of making it necessary for the child to give more
detail in his talk is to help him to make a comparison—by
directing his attention particularly to differences as with Harry
as he looked at a snow-storm novelty:

Harry: I've got one of them.
Miss B: Is it just the same as this?
Harry: No—no it isn't.
Miss B: How is it different?

Harry: Mine has a cowboy and an Indian in and this one has got Father Christmas and some balloons.

Miss B: Are all the balloons just the same colour?

Harry: No—they're all colours—that's blue, and there's a yellow and red—see.

Children need help not only to concentrate on details within the present situation, but also to retrieve detail from an earlier experience which will add meaning to the present experience. Language serves the extremely important function of allowing the user to represent a past or remote, and the anticipated event so that it can be considered within the framework of the present. Peter, for example, ponders on the imminent visit to see his grandmother. The display on the table of birthday cards brought by another child serves to project him over distance to his home, into preceding events and then to look forward to a visit which has not yet taken place.

Peter: And I'm going to see my nan.

Miss T: Are you?

Peter: And we've got a cake —

Miss T: Oh—that sounds good to me.

Peter: Yes—my mum maked it.

Miss T: Can you remember how your mum made the cake?

Peter: Yeh—flour and stuff.

Miss T: And some sugar do you think?

Peter: Yeh—and egg—like this.

He demonstrates turning the handle of a whisk.

Peter: And then in. Do like that.

He makes stirring movements.

Miss T: I don't know what that is you're doing.

Peter: Turning that thing round and round in the eggs.

Miss T: The whisk you mean? She whisked the eggs and then put it all in the cake.

Peter: Yes mixed all up—for a birthday cake.

Miss T: So you're taking your nan a mixed up cake—all nice and sticky?

Peter: No—not then. It's a cake—went into the oven.
Miss T: Oh?
Peter: My mum baked a cake—in the oven.
Miss T: So you baked it in the oven and now you're going
            to take it to your gran. I expect she'll like that.
Peter: Yeh—my nan—it's her birthday—for her birthday.
Miss T: I wonder how you'll get the cake to your nan.
Peter: I know—in a box—I'm going to carry it in a box.
Miss T: So you will walk along and carry the cake in a box
            to your nan's.
Peter: No, we'll go on a bus. It's a green one. And we walk
            a bit—down street—and I'll carry it.
Miss T: What will you do when you get to your nan's?
Peter: Give her it—the cake. And she'll have a birthday—
            happy birthday. I'll sing it for her.

Here we see Peter carrying on a sustained conversation which
ranges over past experiences and then anticipates what has not
yet happened. He does not fill in much detail but from being
unable or unwilling to respond to the teacher's approach he has
over a period of weeks built up an expectation about talking
with his teacher and he is gaining some facility in drawing his
absent world into the present through his talk. This is essential first learning before any more complex reasoning becomes
possible.

There are many situations which arise spontaneously which
will provide opportunities for helping children to reason, and
explain, but to rely on opportunities arising naturally might
mean that some children rarely meet such experience. The
teacher needs, therefore, to make sure that for some children
such opportunities will arise from time to time.

Perhaps the easiest kind of situation to exploit naturally, and
also to 'plan' for is one in which the question 'What happens
when —?' can be put. Later when the child recognises what is
expected of him this can be replaced by 'What happens if?' The
question 'What happens when?' allows the child to experiment
to find the answer and for many children who have not been
expected to think in this way at home, there will be a very real
need to ponder upon what actually does happen, and to register

this through talk, before he will be able to predict the outcome when the question is put in the form 'What happens if?'

'What happens when you mix your red paint with some blue paint?'
'Are you going to do it now—what's happening?'
'What happens when you paint with water?'
'What happens when you put the cork in water?'
'What happens when you trickle some red paint into the water?'
'What happens when you put your ball at the top of a slide?'
'What happens when you roll the dough?'

It is impossible to give a list of all the situations in which a 'What happens when?' kind of exploration can take place. Every such exploration becomes an opportunity for the child to talk about the cause and its effect. Later on many of these same situations will offer the teacher an opportunity to help the child understand why things happened the way they did, and later still to delay activity and predict, for example, 'What will happen if I mix salt with water?' or 'What will happen if I put a big brick on top of the tower?'

The problem for the teacher is not only one of anticipating the right moment at which a question might be asked, for a good deal of sensitivity is needed to judge the moment at which the child can really attend to the question, but also of knowing just what to do in order to help the child to arrive at a satisfactory answer.

It is often difficult for the teacher to judge whether the inadequacies of the child's reply are due to his limited understanding of the question, or his limited knowledge from which the answer must be drawn. The teacher may repeat the question, simplify the language if it is possible, or ask subsidiary questions which aim at helping the child to arrive at the answer. Such supporting questions would offer the child clues to the content expected in the answer and lead him to give an adequate answer.

Discovering the answer to 'What happens when —?' often leads to a closer examination of a situation which is familiar but not thoroughly appreciated. For example, consider Jean's problem when she was in the water play corner and Mrs N came along and said 'Would you like to make the water a nice colour Jean?' Jean nodded and smiled:

Mrs N: Come and choose the colour then.
Jean: This one.

She points to the red colouring.

Mrs N: What colour are you choosing?
Jean: I'm going to make it red—I like red.
Mrs N: What will happen if you put a drop of red into the water?
Jean: The water'll be red.
Mrs N: Will a drop make *all* the water red?
Jean: Yes.
Mrs N: Are you quite sure?

Jean nods.

Mrs N: How big is a drop?
Jean: It's little—very little.
Mrs N: Put a drop in and see what happens.

In this case Jean's difficulty does not seem to be that she had not understood what was asked of her. The problem could have occurred if she had not understood *drop* or *all*, but this does not seem to be the case. It seems more likely here that Jean's knowledge of water may not be adequate, or if it is, that she is not bringing her knowledge to bear on the problem. In this case the experience of adding a drop of red colouring to a trough full of water, discussing the way in which the colour gradually spread until it was hardly to be seen as red, adding drop by drop until the water became faintly pink would be an essential experience for being able to answer the question. It may be that Jean had in fact seen the pink water, but had not had her attention focused on the problem before. In this case her teacher helped her to a new awareness of her experience.

Making something happen and then watching and talking about it makes a situation which is likely to be productive for using language both for description and for relating the cause with its effect. It is also useful because it creates a situation in which the child can be helped to catch on to the meaning of the question 'Why?'

The reader may feel that the question 'Why?' is not one with which the young child needs to be made familiar, for somewhere between about two and a half years of age and three and a half years, some children begin to use 'Why?' with a tedium that irritates the adult.

Two things are clear from the typical 'Why?' asked by three-year-olds. First it does not hold the full meaning of 'Why?': it is not really asking for explanations, but for more information or just more talk. Since mothers do respond with explanations, at least until they tire of trying to find answers, the meaning of 'Why?' gradually emerges for the child, because the adult treats the question as a genuine 'Why?' question.

The difficulty for many children may be that the kind of experience they have when they ask 'Why?' does not help them because the answers it brings are limited to non-explanatory statements, for example, 'because,' 'because I say so,' 'because it is,' 'because you must.' A reply of this kind centres the child's attention on to the fixedness of things rather than on reasons and causes: it does not help him to understand the causal relationship that 'Why?' infers, and the kind of access to information that it can provide him with. So he may learn not to use 'Why?' because it brings no satisfaction for his curiosity. He may not become familiar with answering the question 'Why?' either because reasons are rarely sought from him and if they are, he will tend to reply in the way in which his own questions have been answered.

If the child is to learn the meaning of 'Why?' then he needs to be placed in situations where the meaning of 'Why?' is not only demonstrated, but where he is positively encouraged to use it himself. We may often see that the child is not able to give the kind of answer needed, and the teacher may need to offer to him a model as it were. For example, 'Why doesn't it go red? It's because there's a lot of water and only a tiny drop of red. When the red spreads into *all* the water there isn't enough to make the water even a little bit red. It would need much more red to make the water turn red.'

But helping the child to understand what is happening is

much more than asking 'Why?'; it is a matter of centring on his problem and helping him to work through it, as for example, one sees when five-year-old Paul talks with the teacher about a top as it spins:

Miss Y: Where are all the colours now do you think?
Paul: Gone—they've gone away.
Miss Y: Have they really gone away?
Paul: No but you can't see them.
Miss Y: The colours are really still there, do you think?
Paul: Mm. 'Cos you can't see them.
Miss Y: The colours are still on the top, but we can't see them. I wonder why can't we see them?
Paul: It's going too fast. You can't see them because it's going round fast.

The top loses speed.

Miss Y: Look—what can you see now?
Paul: The colours again—red and blue and all colours.
Miss Y: Why can you see them now?
Paul: Because it's nearly stopped—it's going slow—you can see them.
Miss Y: What did it look like when it was going round fast?
Paul: It just looked like lines—sort of white and black wasn't it?

Using the question 'Why?' not only acts as an invitation to examine events closely as above, it also is a way of helping the child to reflect upon his own feelings and impressions.

He may be pressed to consider his feelings about people, for example:

'Why do you say you don't like Tommy?'
'Why do you think the story's horrible?'

Helping the child reflect on his own inner feelings is an important matter. Equally important is that 'Why?' can also invite him to project into the feelings of others, and so, perhaps, help him to understand them better:

'Why is Johnnie cross with you do you think?'

Just as important as understanding the kind of invitation that 'Why?' offers, is understanding the meaning of 'How'. Again, the meaning is at first ambiguous to the child and he needs to meet it often, with the answer following it, to help him catch on to the meaning:

'How can you get to the top of the slide? Here you are—climb up the steps—that's how to get to the top, isn't it?'
'How does the hamster eat his biscuit? He holds his biscuit in his front paws—isn't he clever? That's how he eats his biscuit.'

This kind of demonstration of meaning is intuitive on the part of the teacher and it clearly has its dangers. It is very tempting to do the talking for the child, particularly when he hesitates or looks uncomfortable. Judgement about how he can be helped most effectively can only come from the accumulated knowledge the teacher has of his behaviour in other situations.

There are many opportunities in the general activity of the classroom to help the child to understand what is expected of him when the question 'How?' is asked, and when he grasps the meaning, then it serves to invite him to recount the way in which something happens, either the way in which he has made or done something, or the way in which something works that he can see and follow quite easily:

'Come and tell us how you made your boat.'
'I like your house, can you tell me how you made it?'

both ask the child to think back over his actions and then retell in sequence.

One of the problems of asking 'How did you?' when the object of the question is at hand is that a quite sensible and appropriate answer is 'Like this—look' and the child can point to the actual construction. To avoid the demonstration 'Look—like this,' the child may be invited to move away from the actuality, to tell someone else what he has been doing. He will have a recent experience of how he actually worked and may struggle to give a detailed account which can be rewarded by the listener finally asking to be shown the results.

Some 'How?' questions, whether posed by teacher or child, may first need an investigation to discover the 'How?' of things. The teacher will probably quite frequently direct attention to something of interest by asking 'Do you know how it works?' and then encourage the child to examine the object or situation to see how it does work:

> 'How do the pedals on a tricycle make it move?'
> 'How can we get marks off a paper?'
> 'How can we fasten two pieces of wood together?'

Opportunities for questions like these are likely to rise spontaneously in the course of the child's activities. A problem is selected and a 'How?' question can set the child off to seek a solution. First of all he is being asked to predict an outcome and then he can be asked to find out whether what he has said is true.

How can we fasten something together—glue, pins, sticky tape, staples? In thinking about the problem the child of necessity must draw on past experience and make some judgements about what is likely to be useful in this immediate problem. Then he can try out his solution and add to his experience of fastening things together.

So the 'How?' question can lead to prediction and trial. It may also direct attention to a great deal of detail about when and where. The 'When?' question might relate to the order of happenings or to a state or condition being reached, e.g. when it's quite dry, when the water is hot, when I'd fixed the handle. The supplementary 'Where?' question leads to closer attention to the details of position, for example 'along the edge,' 'in the middle,' 'underneath,' or 'at the top,' or to location 'in the box,' 'in the cloakroom,' 'at home in my garden.' These two questions 'When?' and 'Where?' are of course not just to be used as supplementary to 'How?' but are questions that are put because they help the child to refine his meaning in almost any discussion where recounting or prediction is the essence of the talk.

The 'How?' question also becomes very appropriate in many

situations where the child is talking about familiar but not present situations. In this situation 'How?' asks him to go over his memories and to relate them without the presence of the actual situation.

'How did you make your cake?'
'How did you get across that busy road safely?'
'How did you make your tent in the garden?'

Understanding and explaining 'Why?' and 'How?' successfully may lead the child to seek more of the same kind of experience. Thus he may begin to look for new opportunities for discovering how and why things work, and he begins to ask these questions himself, looking for relationships, sequences and causes. This is a self-maintaining spiral as it were, leading him to examine, to seek to understand the world as he finds it, leading perhaps to self-initiated learning.

There are other signs that we might look for when we talk with the child in order to judge whether he is in any way reflecting on his experiences. It is very characteristic of the young child's talk that he makes assertions without apparent awareness of the many ways in which his statement could be challenged. As he learns that other people may have a different viewpoint or interpret a situation rather differently, he becomes less certain and indicates by what he says that he acknowledges that there is room for doubt and that other interpretations might be possible. Consider the following responses from two children who were asked what an outline drawing of a figure running might be about.

Jan: He's running fast to get away.
Micky: I think he might be running away from someone, because he's done something naughty perhaps. There might be somebody after him, trying to catch him. But he might be just running 'cos he's late for school or to catch a bus or something like that.

The first reply is in the form of a statement which appears to admit no other solution. The second answer is full of tentativeness, indicating that the speaker is aware that any of these alternative interpretations are possible and, perhaps many others.

We have quoted the responses of two seven-year-old boys here to illustrate the kind of language that would indicate that the child is adopting an attitude of reflection about his experiences, that is, that he is oriented or disposed to reflect upon what he sees and hears and to consider a wide set of alternative interpretations that can be drawn from the clues which are present.

At the ages of three and four, such behaviour is just beginning to appear in some children. 'I think,' for example, is a gambit which some children learn early and at first there may be no intention to modify the meaning of what follows. Since it is likely to be matched quite frequently with another 'I think' from the listener however, in time it might begin to function to allow the interpretation 'This is my view, I know, and you may think something quite differently about it.' Here we see a form of speaking which may be learnt almost as a mannerism from the parents but which may gradually help to establish a disposition to reflect on experiences.

Words like 'perhaps,' 'might,' 'would,' 'could,' 'should,' 'may,' however, come generally rather later. At first they are taken as cues from the speaker. For example, listen to this five-year-old talking about a picture of a pedestrian crossing, with traffic on all sides and a boy about to cross:

Miss Y: What might this little boy be going to do?
Tom: He might be going to run across the road,
Miss Y: What might happen do you think?
Tom: The bus driver might not stop and the boy might get knocked down.
Miss Y: And what then?
Tom: He might have to go to hospital. You do if you have an accident.

Here Tom is taking up the adult's 'might': this serves to make his statements sound tentative. Without 'might' his statements would have been assertions, e.g. 'He is going to run across the road.' Because the child does this, however, he often has returned to him other alternatives, as is the case in the following example:

Miss T: What do you think might be happening here on this picture?

Mary: Well the mother might be telling the little girl to wash up.

Sally: Or she might be saying thank you.

Mary: Or she might just be washing her hands.

Children are helped to arrive at the meaning of some words and phrases for which explanation is impossible by the way in which they are used by others. If the teacher is alert, and notes a child using such words she will be able to play back to him information that will increase his understanding: it will also provide her with a mental note, or a jotting in a record, that such words are being used by a child and that this is a sign of growing maturity of language, and possibly also of the underlying thoughts.

But it is not only the use of words which are associated with the reasoning mode and with uncertainty or tentativeness which are useful indicators of a child's thinking; many new words that are introduced by the teacher, by other children, in stories or in television programmes may become vehicles which allow an exploration of meaning at some depth. We have given an example in which the meaning of the word 'passenger' was explored, as the children played at travelling on a bus. Such opportunities can be made to occur frequently if the teacher is alert to the direction of meaning in a child's play and activity and if she is sensitive to the appropriate moment for introducing a particular word, or drawing attention to the word another child has used.

Where attention is already built in to the situation by the intrinsic interest of their play, concentration can be maintained as the meaning of words are explored. But such strategies on the part of the teacher will only be successful if talk with her adds to the children's pleasure in their play. Once the questions become tedious, then children may begin to avoid catching the teacher's attention. So the teacher must be ready to abandon such efforts before the child's interest in the talk begins to wane

It is clear that some children do become fascinated by the meaning of new words and then may begin to initiate the game themselves.

There are many words which hold little interest for the child but which help to lead to the differentiation of meaning. They may act in the double role of allowing more precise expression of thinking, but also in reverse, promote a new precision in thinking. Amongst words of this kind are the prepositions which allow the expression of rather fine shades of meaning. How is the child to learn the difference between, for example:

1   At the bottom of the cupboard.
2   Below the cupboard.
3   Underneath the cupboard.

Only use and demonstration of meaning can help him to understand the differences in the meaning of these terms.

Talking clearly aids the expression of thinking, and perhaps frequently the very use of talk initiates and refines the child's thinking. When the teacher is listening to the child's talk she must choose whether to intervene or not, she must choose the point and the way in which the child is to be helped to think and think again. Such strategies, in time, might help to produce an inclination on the part of the child to pursue this kind of inner activity and its outward expression through talk because the world begins to appear as a fascinating place which seems to come more and more under control as more knowledge of it is acquired; that is because the meaning it holds for the child is extended.

Chapter 9

Talking and Imagining

Young children can often be seen to be using language for reflecting imaginative experiences which are developed through play. Often the evidence that play is being used in this way comes from seeing the child manipulate materials in certain ways, perhaps with accompanying noises. The child lines up his bricks and pushes them along, making 'train' noises. The observer interprets this as symbolic play. Once beyond the limits of what the materials can represent, however, the imaginary situation must be established through language if others are to share in it.

All children, it seems, play at this level of representation: they take bits of wood and call them boats, or swords or people. Not all children, however, extend their games to creating vivid imaginary situations. It seems likely that those children who find it easy to slip into the 'let's pretend' frame of reference have learned to do it as the result of direct encouragement from a very early age onwards.

We can see that play of this kind leads the child to express ideas through language. If he wants others to join in his game then he must try to be explicit. Children who are self motivated because of the enjoyment they get from this kind of play are therefore providing themselves with a need to describe and explain what their materials and actions represent. This would seem therefore to be a very natural source of impetus to use language. The materials which are most helpful in stimulating the use of the imagination are those which by their form do not impose ideas on the children, but leave them free to impress their ideas on to the materials. Thus a few large boxes and planks in the playground or classroom may become buildings, ships, or vehicles, caves or prisons, changing their usefulness as the ideas within the play change.

We should not assume, however, that because most children embark on imaginative play readily, that the resulting activity will ensure much depth of thought, or representation of ideas in language. Because the materials are there, once they have been named and the scene set, the play may go on just at the concrete level of the here and now representation. And this level of play is worth-while and helpful to the child for several reasons, but not because it necessarily challenges his intellect or his developing skills in the use of language. What it produces is a situation which, because of the self-imposed nature, may be relied upon to maintain the child's interest and involvement and readiness to reach out to new ideas presented in this context. Let us examine an episode of children's imaginative play with the construction materials.

The children have taken two large boxes without lids, and placed them on their sides with uncovered tops facing and at an angle. Over this they have thrown a dust sheet so that they now have a refuge large enough for three children to move about within. To begin with, the construction was to be a 'hide-out' for the baddies:

Dave: Come in, John, come in.
         Give me that thing.

He points to a short plank and John passes it to him.

John: What's it for, Dave?—what's it for?
Dave: To fasten us in—so they can't get us.
John: Right—they can't get us can they?—not in here, can they?
Dave: The sheriff will come and—and get us out—shoot us out.
John: I'll be the sheriff.

He climbs out and deepens his voice.

John: I'm going round here to shoot you. Come on out—I'll shoot you.
Dave: I'll shoot you first.

Both boys make shooting noises and flop as though hit and then go on pretending to shoot. Two other small boys come and stand watching them. Mrs S comes up and also watches for a moment.

John: You see—he's a baddie in there. I'm going to shoot him.

Mrs S: You're shooting him. Do we really shoot people who are just bad?

John: Well—not really. He's a bad cowboy.

Mrs S: Is he? What kind of bad things had he done?

Dave: This baddie has been killing people—robbing them and killing them.

Mrs S: What did he do when he robbed the people?

John: Well—well—he would —

Dave: I know, he jumped out on them—on his horse.

John: And then shooted at them—and take their things.

Mrs S: What might happen then?

Dave: He might kill them.

John: He'll leave them sometimes.

Dave: I know—he takes their horse—and leaves them.

Mrs S: That's a bit dreadful isn't it? How can he manage without a horse?

Dave: Perhaps he'll die.

John: But he could walk.

Mrs S: And what would happen then?

Dave: Tell the Sheriff and they'd all go after the baddie.

Mrs S: Is that what this baddie has done?

John: Yes and I'm going to get him now and put him in prison.

Dave: Take him to jail you mean.

Mrs S: To jail—is that different from prison?

Both boys look at her.

Mrs S: What's a jail?

Dave: It's where you put baddies in prison.

Mrs S: So it's the same as a prison is it?

John: Well it's where you lock up people—both—isn't it?

This episode shows how the level of thinking and of talking changed as the teacher moved in to talk with the boys. A similar change might have taken place at some point without the teacher's intervention, but it is more likely to occur when the teacher stops to see what is happening: children build up expectations about the teacher and where they experience this kind of interest and discussion regularly, they very often meet the teacher half-way by making explicit a notion which otherwise might not have been realised. It is true, of course, that if the teacher makes too many demands for them to divert from their exciting play for a rather tedious discussion, the children may display a resentment at the intrusion. This is a delicate role to play in helping the child to deepen his thinking through his play and to live his imagined experiences more fully.

The greater benefits that such play brings to children may be at a different level, perhaps in the way it helps the child to project into the lives of other people, and into seeing themselves in relation to other people. Thus as they take on the roles of some other person, a child can be helped to explore another's point of view.

Perhaps in the following episode, Jenny does in fact experience something of the feelings of an older person as she plays grandmother to a group of her play fellows who lie close together on the floor in their pretend bed.

Jenny: Now be quiet children. Go to sleep.

Peter: I don't want to go to sleep.
I'm going to be the bad man that comes and frightens you.

Jenny: But don't you know your mother said you'd to go to sleep now.

Jill: Can I have a drink of water Granny?

Peter: Yes we want a drink of water Granny.

Jenny: Will you go to sleep if I get you one—will you?

Jill: I don't want to be the little girl any more.

Jenny: Oh, you are naughty.
(*to the teacher*) Aren't they naughty—they've run away now.

Miss L: Yes they are.
What do you think it's like to be grandma?

Jenny: It's all right really. 'Cos you only have to come when the mother goes out.

Miss L: Oh why's that?

Jenny: She's got no children 'cos she's old.

Miss L: But has she had a child, if she's a grandma?

Jenny: Yes. But they're all grown up aren't they. She doesn't have to look after them now.

Here we can see that the game of being grandma was not far from the child's real experiences and perhaps the experience helped her to work out the problem that grandma has when looking after her.

Often when we talk of children using imagination we are thinking of the fantasy play that some children engage in so easily and frequently. In this kind of activity the child draws the content from what he has been told, stories he has heard, and television programmes he has watched.

The mixture of cowboys, Indians, robbers, spacemen, witches, fairies, jungle life, becoming animals, adventures on the sea, on mountains or in the desert, draw their information from reports of the actuality as well as from tales created about them. For the child there is little difference perhaps between making his fantasy play about family life, fire fighting, witches, robbers, or fantastic creatures, until he is challenged about the real existence of characters like those he creates. The potential of these situations for thinking away from the immediate, real situation is endless, because the situation exists only in the child's mind, with the help, perhaps, of a few props, a hat, or a cloak, or other material which is used to represent the character. For others to share his ideas they must be expressed through his talk.

Often children who can play at this level need very little support from the teacher; a question that suggests another possibility, supplying a detail that makes the play more vivid, posing a problem for consideration, any of these offered at a point where interest might be waning, or conflict seems likely to disrupt the play, might sustain the fantasy experience. The problem is that intervention might curtail the children's own imagining, and listening first to their talk helps the teacher to decide whether intervention would deepen or destroy the experience.

Using the imagination is something that we would wish to encourage in all children, not only because of the pleasure the child can draw from this kind of activity, but because of the kind of thinking that it allows him to pursue.

Those children who already project readily into imaginative play and imaginative thinking have learnt to do this from an early age because adults and older brothers and sisters have made suggestions and demonstrated how to play and think in this way. Such help depends very largely upon talk for making ideas explicit and so this kind of experience is developed through talking: at the same time an inclination to seek and recognise opportunities for such projection is induced which becomes a way of working out ideas which do not necessarily have to be realised in play activity.

Many children, however, have not learned to think and play in this way except at a rather crude level. All children will get much enjoyment from imaginative or fantasy play which demands no more than making appropriate noises, moving in ways characteristic of the people they represent, for example, galloping round and waving sticks for swords, or making the sound of guns. This kind of activity is worth while if only for the pleasure that children get from it, but we should recognise that at this level it may not be extending either their thinking or their talking in any way.

If we feel that all children should be helped to project and explore ideas and situations more fully through the imagination then those children who have not had this kind of experience in their homes, and for whom therefore it is an unknown way of behaving, will depend largely on the teacher for the stimulation and support from which it can be learnt. This may present a very real problem to the teacher if there are few children in the class who are able to initiate imaginative play at this more thought demanding level, and even these children will need her interest and support to sustain play of this kind. But at least those children are likely to respond to her efforts because they know what is expected from them. Those who are unfamiliar with the role of the adult who enters into their play may receive the teacher's efforts with puzzled looks and even a wary withdrawal. They may stop their activity for a short while as though considering the situation, and then without saying anything, or by making a remark which virtually dismisses her intervention, return to the manipulative level of handling toys and materials, or continue play which merely imitates the superficial behaviour of the characters they portray.

Such interventions often produce little response in the way of conversation, and it may need regular and persistent effort on the part of the teacher before children begin to respond in what the teacher feels is an appropriate way. The example given below was by no means the first occasion on which Miss J had tried to encourage Jim and Leslie to extend their usual manipulative, or robust physical play to a fuller use of the imagination.

Jim and Leslie, two four-year-olds, were pushing cars vigorously about the floor making appropriate noises. There was little talk going on between them except for an occasional instruction or comment. Miss J moved to a small chair beside them and watched for a short while.

Jim: Mine's going up this hill, Leslie—brr-brr—and down to the bottom—crash—boom.
Miss J: Where are your cars today, Jim?

Jim sits back on his feet and looks at her whilst Leslie continues pushing his car round.

Miss J: Where is your car going, Leslie?

Leslie stops and holds his car up for her to see.

Leslie: It's not a car—it's a van—see.
Miss J: Yes—I see—well where's your van going today?
Leslie: Don't know—somewhere.
Miss J: It might be going to your house—and Jim's—or mine. What has the driver got in his van?

Leslie opens the van door.

Leslie: There's nothing in it.

Miss J: Can you pretend it has something in? What kind of a van could it be?

Jim: It could be the tele-van.

Leslie: No—it's not the tele-van—it's too big.

Miss J: Could it be the bread van coming round with the bread?

Jim: It is the bread van like what comes down our street.

Leslie: Yes it is—bringing the bread—bringing it to the houses.

Miss J: Will you bring me some bread when you come down my street?

Leslie: Doesn't come down this street.

Miss J: Just pretend I mean. Pretend this is the street your van is coming to and I'm a lady living in a house in that street. Can I have some bread, please, when you come?

Jim: Yes she can—pretend, Leslie—you take bread in your van—what can I take in mine?

Miss J: What other vans come round your street?

Jim: I know I'll be the van what brings potatoes and apples and things.

Miss J: That's a good idea.

Leslie: I'll have some bananas from your van.

Jim: Right—I'll bring them.

Leslie: And oranges I want.

Miss J: Your van's bringing fruit, Jim, is it? Anything else— have you some potatoes?

Jim: Yes—a lot.

Leslie: I'm the breadman coming with my van.

Miss J: I'd like some bread and I'd like some oranges and some potatoes as well when you come down my street.

Miss J worked hard for the next few minutes asking the boys to bring different goods to her pretending to pay for them. She then led talk around to where the vans would get their supply from. There was a short discussion about a bakery and making bread, and then about the fruit market. From there she involved herself further with the play, and the boys in turn went to get supplies for their vans, talked about it with Miss J as though it were really happening until a situation developing in another part of the room drew her attention and she had to leave them.

Perhaps some would feel that Miss J had intruded unnecessarily in the play of these two boys. We have a feeling that children should be left to themselves once play is under way. We see play as an opportunity for the child to work out various kinds of problems of an emotional and social nature and feel that the teacher's intrusion is unwarranted. And indeed we so often see evidence that this is the case that we would not wish to give the impression that we are not in sympathy with this view. Children who are pressed into certain ways of behaving and who find it difficult to succeed, children who find accepting the new baby, or mother's absence from home, or competition with a younger or older brother or sister, intolerable, or who for a variety of other reasons are finding life difficult, can be seen to be meeting and working through these problems in play. This does not mean, however, that the teacher should turn her back on this play, feeling that it is best to be allowed to develop without interruption. If the teacher does not intervene, it will be because this is a conscious decision that the child is gaining needed satisfaction from what he is doing. Sometimes the teacher will intervene, however, either because she sees that the play is becoming in some way overwhelming for the child, or because she feels that a word or two would move the play into something which would be more satisfying and produce deeper thought.

The teacher has the double job of keeping an eye on the child's general social and emotional growth, and on his intellectual development. If she consciously takes a decision not to intervene because the child is getting satisfaction at the emotional and social level, she will also at some point consciously take the decision to move in to help the child use his experience for promoting his intellectual development.

It is true that for some children the home has already extended their talking and thinking, and perhaps their emotional and social development is less mature. In such a case the teacher is clearly right to give higher priority to helping the child to gain emotional and social growth from his experiences in school.

It is also true that some children have emotional and social problems which have been established as a result of their experiences at home which will provide a sort of blockage to developing skills of thinking and talking. Again the teacher will be right to be giving the child help in overcoming his problems, but she will also be seeking further advice and will be discussing perhaps, the child's problems with his mother.

We have digressed for a while because it seems important to establish that although the teacher will often be allowing the child to proceed with his play without any interruption she will do so because she has decided that for this child, at this time, such uninterrupted play is most important: but she will always keep an eye on the way his play develops, ready to change the decision should the situation alter.

The above paragraph may be interpreted by the reader as meaning that the teacher must do the impossible, know what every child is doing every moment of his time in school. This is the ideal kind of staffing arrangement to have, where the number of children in a group is small enough for the teacher to be aware of, if not actually involved in, what the child is doing and know what benefit he is deriving from his experiences all the time he is in school.

Without such conditions it is clear that in any case the child will have ample opportunity for uninterrupted play, for the teacher will be taking decisions all the time according to the priorities guiding the use she makes of her time. Where there are many children in the class whose homes have not provided them with a disposition to use play for extending the imagination, and to use talk for promoting the activity, then the dilemma will be not whether to intervene in the child's play or not, but how best to deploy her time amongst so many children whose needs for the stimulation of their intellect are likely to be met only by regular and sustained experiences of talking with the teacher.

But imagining is not confined to imaginative play. The above episodes have shown children re-experiencing something with which they have become familiar, although perhaps through stories and television and not actual experience. A great deal of imagining of a rather different kind can go on as the child tries to wrestle with a problem that he or one of his playmates or his teacher, has posed. Tim was looking at the fishes in the tank eating the food as it floated on top of the water:

Tim: They're eating it look.
Miss Y: They must be hungry.
Tim: Will they grow fat if they eat a lot?
Miss Y: I expect so.
Tim: Will they get bigger and bigger?
Miss Y: Do you think they will?
Tim: Yes they'll get bigger and fatter until they're as big as that.

He indicates the tank.

Miss Y: If they all grew so big they would be a bit crowded.
John: They couldn't get so big—not all of them.
Miss Y: Oh?
John: Not all of them—'cos they'd get big—and push. If they all got big —
Miss Y: How big could they get?
Tim: One like that.

He indicates a section of the tank.

Tim: And one there like that.
John: There wouldn't be room for those two little ones—they'd be pushed out.
Miss Y: Wouldn't they be growing too?
Tim: They could only get so big—and then they couldn't fit.
Miss Y: Could they really grow so big?
John: Not really—wouldn't be any water for them. But they might grow so big.

He indicates a smaller size.

This little bit of reasoning really begins as an exercise in imagination but finishes with recognition of the reality of the situation and a logical solution. There was a point at which the solution that the imagination allowed was recognised as impossible.

Many opportunities arise in which children can be given experience of trying to solve problems in the imagination. It is true that often the solutions the young child will offer are neither logical nor possible. Sometimes this fact in itself affords another opportunity to help the child think through the problem, and if in the end he does not arrive at a solution, but only discovers that his solution is not practicable, nevertheless he has applied a strategy that will sooner or later bring logical and possible solutions.

The adult who stimulates such discussion, or who follows the lead of a child who finds this an interesting and generally rewarding way to satisfy his curiosity, may often feel at a loss because the questions touch on areas of knowledge with which he is not familiar.

For example, James was looking through the window and could see a crane on the top of a tall building in the distance. He pointed to it and started up the following conversation:

James: Hey look—look at that right on top—Miss T look at it.

Miss T: Where are you looking? Let me see.

James: There—on the big building—on the top. There's something on the end of it.

Miss T: Oh, yes—I see. You mean the crane don't you?— On top of the block of flats behind the church? Is that what you're looking at?

James: Yes—a crane. It pulls things up—I've seen one.

Miss T: Where have you seen a crane working?

James: Saw one with my dad.

Bobby: I've seen one—I've seen one—by the road over there.

Miss T: What was the crane doing when you saw it?

James: Me and my dad we watched it.

Miss T: What did you see it doing?

James: There was a big—a big round—long thing.

Billy: They're big pipes—aren't they?

James: Putting them in the road.

Miss T: Oh—I remember, you mean where they're laying the new drainpipes under the road. They are big ones.

James: And the crane has to lift them—and—and it puts them down into the big hole, doesn't it Bobby?

Bobby: The crane holds it and the man turns it. And then another man shouts.

Miss T: Do you know what he shouted?

Bobby: He shouted 'Down, down.'

James: Yes he does—and then the pipe goes right down the big hole.

Miss T: What do you think the crane is doing up on top of the flats?

James: Lifting big stones.

Bobby: I don't know how it gets up there.

Miss T: I don't. How do you think it could get up there?

James: They'd have to pull it up.

Miss T: How would they do that do you think?

Bobby: They could do it with another crane.

Miss T: Another crane? How would they get that up there?

James: A big lift—on a big lift.

Miss T: Where would the lift be?

James: Inside—I've been in one.

Bobby: We've got one too where I live.

Miss T: Could you get a crane in your lift do you think?

Bobby: No—it's too little.

Miss T: Do you think they could get the crane up in a lift?

James: I don't know how they could get it up.

Miss T: Can you think of any other way of getting something big up there?

James: They'd have to drop it on top—I think.

Miss T: How do you mean James?

James: An aeroplane could drop it down.

Miss T: What do you think Bobby—could an aeroplane drop the crane on top of the building: what would happen?

Bobby: It'd go crash.

James: And it might miss and fall down on the street.
Bobby: And hit the people and the cars.
Miss T: Could anything put the crane on top of the building from the sky, from above I mean?
James: A chopper could—I've seen it on tele.
Miss T: What could?
James: A chopper.
Bobby: It's a helicopter he means—it could.
Miss T: Perhaps it could—why could a helicopter do it and not an aeroplane?
James: Because a helicopter can go up and down—straight —like this—an aeroplane goes like this.

He demonstrates different movements of take-off.

Miss T: So perhaps a helicopter did put the crane on top. What do you think?
James: Yes.
Bobby: No—I don't know—not a helicopter—but I don't know how.

In this conversation there is in the first place an anchor in the real experience of seeing a crane in the street operating. But after that the two little boys try to imagine how the crane might have got on to the top of the building. They had no experience of such a happening, neither had their teacher, nor had she ever needed, or had the interest, to discover the answer to such a question. Nevertheless she encouraged the boys to think of ways in which it might have happened and they did in fact draw on their knowledge about aeroplanes and helicopters to reach a solution, through the imagination, that might work. In the end nobody was clear as to whether this was a solution or not, or where the real solution lay. After this the teacher continued the discussion further because the two boys were still interested. They talked about the differences between helicopters and aeroplanes and then went together to find a book with pictures that would show the differences.

Problems of this kind become interesting and rewarding partly because they challenge the adult's thinking as well as the child's. Often a solution cannot be reached by the child without the adult helping him to examine the reality, and challenging him on grounds of feasibility or logicality.

But it is this kind of thinking, and the readiness with which the child can slip into it, that provides a major learning strategy for solving problems and predicting answers at later stages in his development.

Chapter 10

Talking and Learning

There are clearly wide differences between children in what they have learnt before coming to school. Some four- and five-year-olds demonstrate frequently the extent of the general knowledge they have already acquired. Here is a selection from conversations recorded in James' first term in school during which he had his fifth birthday.

About clouds

James: There's water in the clouds because it goes up from the sea.

Mrs G: Yes that's true. Do you know how the water becomes clouds?

James: It's because of the sun. It steams the water and that makes the clouds.

Mrs G: Yes it does, the sun and the wind evaporate the water. How do the clouds turn into rain? Do you know?

James: I think it's because of the cold. When it's cold it turns to water again.

Mrs G: Yes, it's something like that—the clouds are blown over the land and the rain falls down on us, doesn't it?

About places

The children have been told that a visitor to school comes from New Zealand.

James: I know where New Zealand is—it's at the other side

of the world—because I've seen it on my world—
it's at the bottom—it's south.

Talking about the river near his home

James: And our river's called the Aire and it goes all the
         way to the sea.
Mrs G: Have you been on a boat on the river?
James: On a little one—a rowing boat. But where it goes
         at the sea there are great big ships—I've seen them.
Mrs G: Have you? Where did you see them?
James: At the docks—that's on the side of the river.
Mrs G: What else did you see?
James: Some yachts as well—with sails on.

About animals

When looking at a wormery in the classroom.
James: Some other animals live in the ground. Moles do.
Mrs G: Yes they do—have you seen one?
James: Just a picture—I've seen a picture of one. And in my
         Granny's garden I saw something.
Mrs G: Yes?
James: Well—a pile of soil—on the lawn. The moles had
         pushed it up.
Mrs G: Oh—how had they done that?
James: They've big feet—paws you know—and they dig a
         tunnel and push the soil out.

When looking at a picture of farm animals with the teacher.

Mrs G: What does the farmer get from the animals do you
         know?
James: The cow has some milk—in that thing under there.
         And the farmer gets it with a machine. Then—then
         he puts it in bottles with another machine.
Mrs G: What about the other animals? Do they give the
         farmer anything?
James: The hens—they lay eggs—but not that cock. And
         the ducks lay eggs too 'cos I've had one.

Mrs G:	What about this animal?
James:	That's a sheep. The farmer gets that stuff off it.
Mrs G:	The wool?
James:	Yes—and that makes jerseys and socks doesn't it?
Mrs G:	What's the biggest animal you know?
James:	Well—I think—I think an elephant. That's very big —and it lives in hot countries—Africa. But I've seen one.

About trees and seasons

As he shows to his teacher some coloured leaves he has picked up on his way to school.

James:	And the leaves all come off the trees in winter and in spring they grow again.
Mrs G:	Do all the trees lose their leaves in winter?
James:	No some don't—we've got some in our garden that don't.
Mrs G:	Do you remember what they are?
James:	Holly—and some others I can't remember.

About the post

As he watches Mrs G putting a letter into an envelope.

Mrs G:	What happens to a letter when we put it in a post box?
James:	The postman comes and empties it. And then he takes it to the Post Office—and some men sort them all out—where they're to go.
Mrs G:	Do you know what happens then?
James:	Yes it goes in the big bags and they put them on trains—I've seen them. And when they get to where they've got to go the postman takes the letters out to the houses. Sometimes he goes in a red van—but he walks to my house.
Mrs G:	If you send a letter to someone in another country how would that get there—by train?

James: It could go by aeroplane—it says Airmail on the letter so they'll know.

Mrs G: Do letters go by ship sometimes?

James: Yes I think so.

About cars

Looking at Mrs G's car in the playground.

James: Our new car's got the engine in the back and the boot's at the front. Isn't that funny?

Mrs G: It won't have a radiator at the front like mine then?

James: No—it doesn't have a radiator at the back.

Mrs G: Doesn't it? I wonder why?

James: Well you see it doesn't have water to keep it cool—like it goes round the radiator—just air keeps it cool—the engine.

Knowledge of time and clocks

James: When it's time to go home both hands are up at the top aren't they? That's twelve o'clock.

And on another occasion.

James: The little hand says o'clock—look—three o'clock. And the big hand says half past doesn't it?

About shape

James: Well that's a round.

Mrs G: Do you know another name for it?

James: It's a circle, and that's a square.

Mrs G holds a rectangle.

Mrs G: Is this a square too?

James: No it's not—because the sides are not the same. But I can't remember what you call it.

Mrs G: It's a rectangle—and what about these?

James: Those are triangles—and that and that. They've got three sides and I know what you call it when it's got eight sides. It's an octagon.

Knowledge of numbers

As he comes to the milk table with his friends and they take bottles from the centre of the crate.

James: Mrs G we need another milk—we've only got four bottles.

James counts the eight steps up to the slide without any difficulty or mistake.

What shall the young child learn?

James is a normal, well adjusted five-year-old: he talks easily and readily and is generally very friendly towards children and adults. The examples given here are typical of the way in which he talks and the range of topics that he is happy and interested to talk about is wide. Many five-year-olds display a similar readiness to talk and show that they have an immature but developing knowledge on a wide range of subjects.

Is this the kind of knowledge that we would expect children to have by the age of five? As teachers we have an intuitive unease about a child who seems to know too much, unless he displays particular skills by which he can be recognised as a prodigy, in which case we accept it as something to be wondered at. Often teachers, and some parents too, perhaps, find themselves in a dilemma when trying to decide what is suitable learning for the young child to accomplish. Shall we help him to memorise a useful set of facts, the meaning of which he cannot fully understand? Shall we help him to learn labels which are terms associated with particular areas of knowledge, for example, the actual mathematical terms for the shapes the child would be happy to describe in other ways? Shall we help him to learn to count, to recognise coins, to begin to recognise words or even try to help him to learn to read?

This is a real dilemma for the teachers of young children: what is suitable learning for the child between the ages of two and five? We know of the problems some children have when parents set out to teach certain skills, usually reading, writing, and computation, and who exhibit great anxiety and disappointment when the child does not learn successfully. If the child proves to himself, as well as to his parents, that he cannot learn these skills, the problems of convincing him that he *can* learn when he is in school are often insurmountable without special help. So we are perhaps rightly critical of parents who set out deliberately to teach their young children in any formal way because we are only too aware of the problems that failure to meet the expectation of parents creates for the child and subsequently for the teacher.

On the other hand, we are critical of parents if their children have not learnt enough by the time they come to school. We have, it seems, a feeling that some kinds of learning ought to be achieved in the home at an early age, whilst other forms of learning should be left until later or left to the school. We want the child to have learnt to take care of himself and be independent of the adult's attention for his physical needs, and we are indignant if he has not done so. We expect him, too, to have learnt some social skills, particularly about how to get on with other children, to care for toys and equipment, and to recognise the authority of adults, and we think the mother has been negligent if the child has not learnt this.

How does the young child learn?

But how do we regard the kind of learning that James has accomplished by the age of five? Is it a good thing for children to have a wide general knowledge of this kind, and if it is, how is it to be taught? The argument is often advanced that there is so little of early childhood and so much of life to follow, even school life, that early childhood should be allowed to be pressure free, and devoted to doing that which is seen to be the essence of early childhood. But what is it that can be judged to be the natural activity and development which belongs to early childhood? There can be no argument about the fact that the child grows and develops physically, and that he is able to control and direct his own movements more and more successfully during the years between two and five. We would therefore expect a good deal of the child's activity to be directed towards acquiring skills which depend on the control of physical movement. Thus we would expect to see him taking great pleasure in jumping, running and climbing, in balancing and taking aim, in manipulating smaller tools and toys than hitherto, and in gaining mastery over smaller and more intricate movements. We would encourage him to gain such skills by placing materials within his reach which would stimulate such interest and activity.

Socially too, during these years the child is developing as a member of the family. Where he is allowed and encouraged to play a useful part within the family, he shows his ability to learn by undertaking some responsibility for his own cleanliness, respecting the property and rights of other members of the family, and even for doing small jobs about the home which are seen to be helping mother or father. We would see this as natural learning because it involves little formal teaching and is learnt because of involvement in the ongoing life of the family. We would see school as also offering continuous experiences from which such social learning can proceed naturally.

How does the child learn to use language?

We also recognise that early childhood is the period in which the child quite naturally learns to talk. We expect early childhood to be a period in which much learning about speech and language is accomplished, so much so that if a child comes to nursery school, even at the age of three, unable to communicate through speech, we assume that either he must be of low intelligence, or that the home has failed to help him learn to talk. But, apart from efforts to help the child correct errors in articulation or in the simple structures of the language, we would expect that there would be little formal teaching about language or speech, and so we describe this as learning which is natural for the child at that age.

How then does the child have his *natural* language activity in which speech and language are developed? What kind of activities form the basis for his linguistic development, in the same way that running and climbing provide the expression of his physical development. The crux of the matter is that language is the medium of the expression of ideas, and it affords the means of communication. So language is developed in situations in which communication through speech goes on. Talking is perhaps, essential in the first place for the young child as a means of letting people know about his general well-being. But he does not live in a world which is only made up of bed-time, meal-time, and play-time. The world exists outside the family and the family relates to it in many ways. Indeed the world outside is brought within the family by television, newspapers and magazines. So the family is likely to be communicating between its members about aspects of the world which interest or involve them. Communication about matters of this kind are made explicit through speech and also provide language experience for the child.

The family has its own life made up of the relationships between the members of the family, and the general activities which the family pursue. Again, language provides the medium through which communication can go on. It is this activity into which the child is drawn, which, with little formal teaching, provides the matter about which the child wants and learns to communicate. It is not talk for talk's sake, or talk about things which are only considered suitable for communication with the child (although such topics will form a part of the child's experience) that forms the natural experiences in which to establish and practise language: it is everything that goes on which is of interest or concern to the family, and in which he is able to become involved as his skill in interpreting and speaking grows.

Learning by talking

So the child learns to use language in the atmosphere of the home, and if talk in the family includes talk about the weather, cars, travel, plant and animal life, shape and numbers as it does in James' family, and if the child is seen as a developing member of the family, growing gradually, and to be helped, into the interests of the rest, then he is going to begin to form ideas about those things. He cannot talk without learning something about the content of the talk, for this is the goal of communication. Moreover, the more he includes such interests to form the content of his talk, the more information is played back to him from the others because of their own interest: in this way members of the family intuitively teach him about things that interest them.

Nor is all the talk likely to go on at an abstract level. Much of the communication will go on as the activities themselves are underway, or as attention is focused on the real situation, for example, the plants in the garden, the engine in the car. And the one who seeks to communicate is often bound to demonstrate his meaning through directing the attention of his listeners to the particular features about which he is giving information. For example, a discussion of cooling systems is likely to take place when an examination, however superficial, of different cars and their cooling systems is being made.

So long as the child is treated as one to be included in the discussion, and one who is to be helped to understand the information contained in the situation, then he is being provided with opportunities for learning. If all his experiences of talking were unsupported by the actual experience of the things talked about, then much of the talk would be inaccessible as a means of learning. There is likely to be a good proportion of the talk between adults which remains inaccessible to him for this very reason in any case.

Characteristic of the young child's learning is the need for the actual experience, the information that comes to him through senses. Talk alongside this experience may draw his attention to the important aspects of this experience, will demonstrate a relationship, perhaps, or will help him to structure the whole into something which is coherent and meaningful. Talking that is relevant to his experience may then provide the child with a meaning for the experience different from that which it would have had if it had happened without the accompanying talk.

Some limiting conditions for the child's learning

What then shall we consider suitable learning for the child? The answer must surely be that which he is able to acquire from the experiences and talk that might go on around him. Many topics may seem to us less suitable than others, but this may be due more to the kind of knowledge with which we ourselves are familiar or to what we see as worth-while knowledge, than to what may be accessible learning for the child: we would naturally avoid burdening him with information that might be actually disturbing for him. But where his needs as a participator are taken into account, and there is an effort to provide the needed demonstration, and information is given simply in talk, the child may learn much which we may not have considered to be within his reach.

The child's immaturity of thinking, as has been said before, will set a limit on how much he can understand. Much of his experience will go by, leaving only a superficial impression, or partial knowledge, sometimes a set of facts or statements without any underlying structure of understanding except that it is so. Provided that these are sound so far as they go the knowledge is likely to be of advantage to him rather than otherwise.

So from the outset we must accept that the child's learning may go on at different levels of understanding. It would be wrong to exclude as unsuitable learning that which the child can only assume at a superficial level. On the other hand to argue that we could help the child to acquire a lot of knowledge at this superficial level which could lie for some time, perhaps years, waiting for understanding of the underlying structure of the knowledge to be completed, takes no account of the way in which the child becomes involved either through interest, because the topic is presented in a particular way, or through the relationship with members of his family where talking about a topic which may not have intrinsic interest for him is rewarding because of the status it seems to give him when he is able to join in the discussion. If similar involvement can be created in schools then he will indeed pick up a great deal of knowledge from those he talks with. For example, if the teacher has a special interest in natural science, or keeps pets and sees them not just as something for the child to look after but also for him to learn about, the child is likely to build a general store of knowledge about these things which may be at a somewhat superficial level, but which nevertheless can be sound.

Some differences in children's learning

To return to our theme, we can see that children, when they first come to school will have very different collections of knowledge, and we should expect this to be so. Can this in itself explain why children respond to their early school experiences so differently? Why do some children have difficulty in responding to the experiences provided in classes for young children? What are the sources of their problems of understanding? Why are the opportunities for learning in the early years of school so differently used? Why do the experiences we give to young children seem to have different meanings for different children? Is it just that some children have had more experiences than others?

We often talk as though the child from the impoverished home is deprived of experience, and clearly this is not the case in the majority of instances, although it is likely that young children in high flats may actually be deprived of general experience. The child who is free to wander in the street or countryside may meet a variety of experiences that the child kept restricted to the house and garden or yard cannot meet. Yet we would not argue that this would necessarily be to his advantage when he came to school, except perhaps for a certain independence of the adult: and in fact this very independence may provide an important disadvantage since it means he has learned not to seek the help or approval of adults and is not disposed to turn to the teacher except to gain permission to proceed with particular activities.

Understanding the nature of children's learning

As teachers of young children, there are several mistakes we can make about the nature of the child's learning. The first would be to assume that the young child can learn much from talk or instruction alone. He is very much dependent upon sensory experience, that which he can see, touch and handle, for his basic learning.

The second is to assume that the young child can reason about his own learning and can learn because he's decided to: that is that he can learn because he has been persuaded that he ought to learn by his parents or his teacher. This may be the case later on in childhood, but even then motivation of this kind may not be sufficient. Certainly in the child between two and six, though persuasion might produce initial attention, it is not enough to hold it if the following period is tedious or there are obviously other things that attract his attention more. The learning, however, might be quickly accomplished if his interest or involvement with people give him an impetus towards it. This is the crucial question—how is such impetus towards learning stimulated and maintained?

The third mistake is to assume that the provision of particular activities and an environment which is particularly stimulating for the eyes and hands, much to see and much to do, will necessarily produce much learning. We often refer to this as providing a rich environment, and it is usually supported by regular visits outside the school to experience what is happening in the streets, in the park, or at places like the fire-station. Sometimes teachers go to tremendous lengths to provide something novel in the way of experience for their children, for example, a boat or an old car is hauled into the playground or even into the building itself to become the scene of many exciting games.

We must be careful to make our meaning quite clear here. We are not in any way saying that to provide such experiences is not useful, but we should not assume that the child will of necessity learn much although he may enjoy it as a new experience. This is to take too simple a view of how the child learns. A teacher who provides relatively less exciting material may in fact achieve more for the children because of the way in which she uses what she has provided. She will use, for example, the children's experience of streets, shops, traffic, and the park and playground much more extensively as she talks with children, helping them to use or discover their knowledge, and sometimes feeding in new information, perhaps exploring the meaning of a new word. Similarly children may learn much more with the teacher who keeps interesting living material in the classroom or out in the grounds, caring for growing plants, pets of different kinds, providing interesting specimens to look at under a standard magnifying glass and who talks with the child, maintaining and sustaining his interest, than with one who is continually taking children on expeditions to see nature as it is but who believes that to gaze is enough.

Extending meaning by classroom activities—an example

Perhaps to emphasise this point we might contrast the impact of a display, very familiar in many infant and nursery schools, in which many objects are put together which are in various shades of one colour. Some of these are very impressive and quite beautifully done and can be used to stimulate different kinds of thinking. If such a display is put together by the teacher alone, when the children are not present, or perhaps even put together when children are present but not involved in the activity, or perhaps even directed not to be interested in it, then much of its potential as a learning experience is dissipated. The value would be realised as children look for, and bring articles for the table, discussing the articles, their structure and their use, comparing the colours and how and where to put their pieces in particular relationship to one another in the display: to have anticipated the activity by previously placing many articles of this colour about the school to await discovery would ensure that the success of the operation was not placed in jeopardy by the absence of materials to display. Even the background could become the centre of discussion as a small group of children looked with the teacher at a collection of materials from which the background could be selected discussing the advantages of one or another material or colour.

To make such a display without the involvement of children and the spontaneous teaching and learning which could go on around it is to have missed the most important opportunity that it provides. If, in addition to neglecting this period of preparation, the teacher assumes that children will learn much from just being exposed to the visual effect of it then almost all the value of the experience will be lost. How can we tell what impact such a display has had on young children, or even older ones for that matter, if many opportunities are not made for children to talk about it, helping them to make comparisons, noting differences in size and shape and shade of colour, of different effects as the light shines on the pieces and through them. Some children, it is true, will stop and comment and ask questions: they will be the initiators of their own learning. But for the many who have not learnt to respond in this way the whole effort may be just so much wasted energy and neglected opportunity.

The concrete experience, then, is not enough. We must be careful here lest we give the impression that we decry the energy which some teachers put into making their school an interesting place to be in, or into bringing in new and novel objects; or in taking children out in the neighbourhood; such experiences are obviously valuable for all children, particularly if the experience is explored with them through talking together. We only want to emphasise here the mistakes that can be made if the teacher assumes that it is the sensory experience which is the only stuff of learning. Talking is the complementary experience which not only helps the child to examine his experience with awareness of its qualities, but gives the teacher a view of what the child is learning from the experiences she is providing.

Approach to reading and writing

Finally, whilst we are considering what and how the child should learn, we must turn to the vexed question of whether the young child should be taught anything of reading and writing. We have given examples of the kind of knowledge James, a rising five-year-old, had acquired: in addition we should have noted that he could recognise and write his own name, and that he could recognise words on a number of cards that were used at various times for labelling in the classroom (for example, 'hospital,' which was used to rename the home play area), and in addition he could 'read' a number of books where the pictures gave clear clues to what the reading content was. Much of this reading activity was probably based on guessing, but James was learning to use clues to make his guessing more successful.

Was his teacher wrong to allow James to come into contact

with such material and to have acquired such skill? James clearly is ready to learn to read and no doubt his home experience would promote such learning even if the school provided nothing. We have said earlier in this chapter that teachers of young children are right to be wary of imposing on children instruction which cannot be met successfully. We must guard against the child learning that he cannot learn, that is giving him evidence of his failure. On the other hand if we maintain that the child should be encouraged to learn anything that he can that appears to be *natural* learning at that time, and that in a *natural* ongoing environment in which people have interest, exchange ideas, practise particular skills, he shows that he can learn by his own interest and motivation, then he should be encouraged to do this.

In a home where books, newspapers, comics and magazines are being read and the child begins to show this interest as he looks at books, listens to stories, and talks about pictures, where he is encouraged to make a contribution to letters to grandma or friends by enclosing one of his drawings, then he is likely to begin to catch on to what reading and writing is about. His natural home experience is then providing him with a splendid preparation for learning to read and write. If he himself picks up the pencil and says, 'I want to write my name' should parents or teachers persuade him that he is too young? We would ask them not to pursue this if the child demonstrates his inability to succeed, or grows tired of the activity. But if the child persists, and says 'Write I'm coming to see you soon Granny' and then insists on copying it, should we make parents who comply with his wishes feel guilty? Should we disvalue his attempt at learning because we feel the learning was accomplished for the effect it would produce on his parents or his teacher and not because of his intrinsic love of the activity? But so much of the young child's learning is accomplished because he wants to share in adult activities.

We would surely recognise in this kind of behaviour, a readiness on the child's part to respond to the written word, and would perhaps begin to provide short written statements which held interest and meaning for him, perhaps helping him to make a book of his drawings for which he dictated his own captions or story. We would point out notices to him in shops and buses, we would answer his question 'What does that say?'. All this, the reader would perhaps say, is just common sense. It would be just as unfortunate to frustrate the child who is pressing to be included in those who communicate through the written word, as it would be to insist on trying to teach him to read when it clearly has no meaning or interest for him.

The educative environment

If our criteria for deciding whether the child shall be helped to learn to read and write, is to take account of the demonstration of his aptitude and interest, then two questions must be asked.

First, how is the child to demonstrate this aptitude and interest if the environment in which he finds himself offers no opportunities for expressing interest and demonstrating aptitude? Do aptitude and interest just develop without any kind of stimulation? How have children who have aptitude and interest before the age of five, acquired it?

The second question is the important one, since it raises the whole question of the experiences which children have at home which provide a natural development towards communication through written signs. Without any deliberate intention, just because homes are what they are, some provide unavoidable continuous preparation whilst others provide very little. If school for young children is to provide an environment which simulates the educating home, then at least it must provide evidence that reading and writing are a part of the way of living. We should not, because children cannot read, have no written matter displayed, or never draw their attention to the written word. Because they cannot write we should not avoid saying, 'See, I am writing to the milkman to say please leave twenty bottles of milk.' If life in the class for young children does not demand from teachers the same need for writing that their homes provide, we should not consider that we are cheating because we have to set about making writing and reading appear. Nor should we feel guilty because we involve children in talking about things that are written or being read. The life of young children should include the presence of reading and writing and people who demonstrate that they use them. What must be avoided is making the child feel that until he too can do it he is unworthy, or unsuccessful: the expectancy that should be apparent and transmitted to the child is that these skills are useful and bring pleasure and that one day he too will join those who practise and benefit from them.

We must make quite clear that we are not in any way advocating that we should attempt to teach young children to read (although we would add that to prevent children learning to read, who are obviously just on the brink of reading, whatever their age, seems absurd). What we are saying is that for some children the only environment that will offer the basic essential experiences from which reading will develop when they get to the infant school, will be that which they meet in school whether before the age of five or after. It seems common sense to suggest that we should seriously consider what those basic essential experiences are and find ways of providing them in the same way that our own homes provide a preparation for reading for our own young children.

The importance of stories and rhymes

In considering what those basic essential experiences might be, we should not underrate the importance of listening to stories and rhymes. For many children the introduction to stories, rhymes, and books begins at a very early age, as the demands of their older brothers and sisters are satisfied. The baby may be included in this experience long before the meaning for him can be more than a sense of comfort and security, the sound of the rising and falling voice, the turning of pages, and the eyes of other children directed at the story teller. For such children, learning to interpret stories has developed over several years.

It is difficult to judge how much one- and two-year-old children can understand of the stories to which they listen. Rhythm and rhyme seem to bring pleasure at an early age, and we often see this as the young child struggles to interject words at appropriate points. If it means nothing more, he is certainly learning to enjoy the story and rhyme situation even though his understanding of the content may be very limited.

But as the child approaches the age of three, the full meaning of the story will gradually become more and more accessible to him. As he listens to stories he will meet them with many developing skills. He must grapple with a sequence of ideas. He must hypothesise about the meanings of words he has not met before. He must try to project and anticipate possible developments for the story. So his listening and interpretive skills grow and feed into his developing ability to use language.

We should remember, too, that listening to stories provides him with very different experiences from listening to talk. Much talking goes on where meaning is made clear by the situation in which it takes place. The speech itself may not be explicit, it may be hesitant, even fragmentary. Few people talk in a formally 'correct' way: many contractions are made particularly with the negative and within the verb phrase. In talk there is often a distortion in the pronunciation of words which is part of a local or regional pattern.

As children listen to stories, however, they meet another form of the language, as it conforms to the rules and conventions of writing. Well-formed sentences provide a new model, and there will be fewer contractions. The written language will tend to be explicit, the reader will tend to speak more clearly, and the flow will not be interrupted by hesitations and reformulations.

The language of stories may also present the child with new strategies, unusual similies or metaphors, sequences of words included for sound effects, which would be rarely sought in talk. The experience of listening to stories and rhymes gives the child another model of language, one that he associates with stories and which he begins to adopt for the narration of his own inventions.

We can see from this that the experience of hearing stories provides important essential experiences for learning to read. It is more than the experience of seeing black marks on a page imbued with meaning. It is more than seeing pages turned from right to left, or the gesturing finger following the print from left to right. It is essentially familiarising the child with the written form of the language. This will provide him with a basis from which to anticipate what will follow in his reading book, and provide him with a model when he begins to write himself.

Equally important is the fact that listening to a variety of stories extends the child's use of his imagination, and his projection into situations he has never met and into the lives of people he can never become.

For some children such experiences occur regularly every day. Many children, however, will have little background experience of this kind. But the experiences are so important —both for the development of the child's thinking and as a preparation for reading and writing—that stories and rhymes read and told to small groups must find a place in nursery and infant classrooms as essential basic experience.

Communication in the classroom: a way of life

Stories and rhymes, however, are only a part of a way of life that provides essential basic experiences. We are talking about a way of life that stimulates curiosity and problem-solving attitudes, that encourages the use of representation, through both the use of painting and modelling materials and the development of imaginative play, where representation and interpretation go on through role playing and the renaming of play materials and the representation of an imagined scene through the use of language. We are thinking about developing a need to look at books and to talk about pictures through stimulating the child's growing curiosity and interest in them. Above all we are meaning the development in the child of an urge to communicate his ideas to others through talk, through his own pictures, and finally to the urge to fix some of his talk in writing for others to see. These are all activities which develop skills that will be drawn on or will precipitate the child into reading when he meets the written word. They are all activities that depend for their development on the talk between the child and the adult.

We have ranged pretty widely in this chapter on talking, experiencing, and learning. It is clear the young child is dependent on first-hand experience for his learning. The accompanying talk, however, is the means by which his attention is directed towards those experiences, and in communicating the kinds of value and the interpretations that can be set on these experiences. His own questions, and the exchange of information through conversation, provide him with the means of becoming equipped with a new appreciation of what is happening around him.

Chapter 11

Focus on Meaning

Talking to some purpose with young children

And now we are reaching the end of what we set out to say about talking with young children; that is, about the way in which the teacher can seek to promote the use of language by young children for a variety of important purposes.

Our intention in writing this book has been to draw attention to the nature of children's talk, and to children's dependence on adults for initiation into subtle and more complex uses of language. We are seeking to persuade the teacher not to dismiss children's talk as 'just talk,' not to see talk as incompatible with learning. Our plea is that talking should be recognised as providing, for young children at least, the major route to learning. And when we say learning, we are not referring to the learning of language itself but to learning generally. It is the child's capacity for talking that should be used for extending his thinking, for developing ways of using language that will serve him well, and that will provide him with strategies for learning.

There are those who will say that there are more important things to do with young children than badger them into talking a lot: we agree. Such people will say that the social and emotional development of children must be a first priority: we agree. The teacher of young children must see her first responsibility as one of helping children to cope with the separation from home, to adjust to the life of school, to make good relationship with other children and with teachers and other adults in school.

We are quite clear about our priorities, but we must add that in fulfilling these priorities neither the teacher nor the children will remain silent: talking will be an important dimension in helping this adjustment to take place. Indeed, the child's talk will provide important evidence about the state of his acceptance and adjustment. The teacher needs to be very sensitive to the child's problems at all times, and teachers' talk should be a reflection of that awareness. The child who is timid, fearful and shy, may shrink if pressed to talk, his problems made even greater by demands that he is unable to meet. Perhaps we would all recognise the establishment of some relationship with either teacher or another child in which talking can take place, as a sign that such a child is making some progress.

Developing language skills in school

We hope that we have dispelled the fears that some teachers have that we want to introduce formal language lessons for young children, providing patterns of speech to be repeated and drilled, imposing a form which does not arise from a situation which has some intrinsic meaning for the child. We see no place for such lessons, but see the structures of language being acquired because children are motivated to search for an adequate expression for communicating about something which arises from their own interest and involvement.

Imposing talking upon the child which has no relationship to his interests and activity seems to be a sterile approach when the very nature of the child's curiosity and play provide a natural guarantee that talk will arise from situations which already hold his interest and attention; this the teacher can use, even exploit, to lead him to pursue ideas and express them through talking. We are not then recommending that children should be set to practise particular speech structures: we recommend quite the reverse. At this age the child's willingness to be engaged in almost any activity the teacher sets up for him offers all the opportunity the teacher needs for promoting talk which is relevant to the child.

The knowledge and understanding that a child can draw from his immediate contact with the world is limited. Much of the meaning of his concrete and social experiences comes to him through the interpretation set upon them for him by his parents and their associates, brothers and sisters and their friends. Meaning is drawn not just from the way others react to the same experiences but also through the transmission, through talk, of how others receive these experiences. The meaning of his experiences is established gradually during early childhood as a result of the impact which day-to-day living with his family makes on the child. For some children life in school may be an extension of life at home: for others home and school experiences may be quite different, perhaps even conflicting.

Communication and learning in the home

It is easy to oversimplify the situation: clearly it is not the case that there are families which operate in two strikingly different ways and so produce two groups of children with clearly different attitudes and dispositions to use school experience. Many factors combine to produce the character of the environment in which the child grows up: the origins, education and life of the grandparents, the upbringing and education of the parents, the section of the population with which the parents have strong links, the neighbourhood in which they live, the view they take of their children and the purpose they see for childhood, the view they have of education, the hopes they have about their children and the actions they take to achieve these goals, all these will play some part in determining their way of life, their attitudes and values, and the expectations they have about their children's behaviour and their future lives. This results in a wide range of different priorities in bringing up children, and produces no clear division between one way which is clearly favourable for benefiting fully from education and another way which is completely antagonistic to education and which produces children who seem to benefit little from school experience. All that can be said is that these two patterns may represent the extremes between which the majority of families are spread. There is also the personal history of the particular child to be taken into account, his personality and the circumstances which are unique to him, which play a part in the way in which he reacts to his experiences. We make a mistake if we view the child as a completely passive recipient of what his home holds out to him.

Although there is a general tendency to assume that only

those who are really depressed in their living conditions are at a disadvantage in school, many children are in fact at a disadvantage when compared with those for whom the home provides continuous stimulation for the child to learn in a way which is completely harmonious with the goals of education.

It is the pattern of communication and the values that underlie this that influence the child's learning, and it is to these that we must look for explanations of why many children fail to respond in the way we would hope when they first come to school, and indeed, for some, throughout their schooldays. And we should be clear that it is not that children in some families have learned and others have not; it is rather that they have learned differently. Those children whose homes have helped them to become curious, to question, to look for explanations of cause and effect, and processes, to be alert to the range of possible interpretations of experiences, and in general to view the world as offering a series of problems to be solved—these children are likely to find the modern nursery and infant school to be new arenas in which to practise and demonstrate their skills. They find themselves in a world that offers new opportunities and appreciates their efforts.

For others school is a bewildering world of alien people which constitutes a threat to them. The relationship with adults which disadvantaged children have learnt to expect, is one that does not foster explorative uses of language; these children have learnt to look to the adult for instructions, they have learnt not to question but to accept the order of things as they are. What the child has learnt at home is the only frame of reference against which he can, at first, interpret the experience of school. Children come to school differently equipped, and it has different meanings for them.

Teaching the disadvantaged young child

There is at this time a popular view developing that schools fail to value the disadvantaged child and his culture, and to some extent this may be true: the argument that teachers favour the children from families which have similar interests to theirs may be valid, as may the accusation be that we want to turn children into the model that the children of the better educated section of the population present. It is an argument that is likely to confuse the issue, except that it challenges us as teachers to examine our assumptions about what children ought to be able to do when they come to school and what these assumptions lead us to do: we may cherish the already favoured, and neglect those who do not conform to our picture of the child who is eager to learn, and is appreciative of the efforts we make on his behalf.

But this is only part of the argument. Education thrives upon interest in, and involvement in, whatever it is that is to be learned. What is seen to be desirable content for learning may change, but the means of achieving it will be the same. It is the strategies that the children of educated parents have learned that provide them with important means of learning: it is not necessarily the goals of such parents that should be recommended.

If disadvantaged children are to benefit from education, then first of all they need the tools of learning; we are not benefiting them if we allow those tools to remain undeveloped; for whatever purposes disadvantaged children use their skills of learning later, the tools and strategies they need are those which other children are already beginning to develop before coming to school. These are essentially, as we have attempted to show, the skills in using language as a means of examining the detail, the relationships and the structure of the world around them. They are the skills of logical argument, of examining a range of possible solutions to problems, of anticipating and planning, and of framing questions which will bring the kind of information required. These are the tools of thinking: there can be no argument against the need for all to be able to bring such skills to bear upon any topic or problem to which their attention is turned.

The development of such skills in the school is dependent upon a particular kind of relationship between the teacher and the child, one which encourages flexible ways of thinking. The problem is to help children to develop an attitude of inquiry and to view control of themselves as something in which they should participate. This means establishing a relationship with the teacher which they may not before have experienced. Building new attitudes towards experience through the encouragement and understanding of the teacher seems likely to result in new learning skills which will be reflected in their use of language.

We can find no reason to suggest, however, that we should provide a different kind of learning environment for these children. But there will be differences in the way in which we set about helping the child to learn in that environment. First of all the teacher needs to be aware of the skills she is trying to establish in order to build a new alertness in the child to the experiences which school provides. She helps him to reflect on his own experiences, feelings and intentions and to project into the feelings of others. The content of such talk will differ because of what is found to stimulate his interest, and it will be necessary for the teacher to be frequently and directly involved in the child's chosen activities. Essentially she will be helping the child to focus his attention on something that has a potential interest for him. She will use the child's response, his meaning, as a starting point from which talk might lead into deeper and more complex thinking.

For the disadvantaged child the teacher may be the only person he will meet who can promote the development of new uses of language, who can help him to see that the communication of his ideas is worth while.

If the child is to be helped to discover new meanings for his experiences it will come through those relationships with the teacher which reward his efforts to communicate, since this opens up opportunities for the teacher to extend the child's thinking.

The focus on meaning necessitates insight not only into the child's and the teacher's talk but embraces the purpose of all our activities in school.

Bibliography

Almy, M. (1966). *Studies of Young Children's Thinking.* New York: Teachers College Press.

Baldwin, A. L., and Frank, S. M. (1969). "Syntactic Complexity in Mother-Child Interactions." Paper presented at meeting of the Society for Research in Child Development, Santa Monica, Calif. Reported in C. B. Cazden (1972).

Bereiter, C. E., and Englemann, S. (1966). *Teaching Disadvantaged Children in the Preschool.* Englewood Cliffs, N.J.: Prentice-Hall.

Bernstein, B. (1971). *Class, Codes and Control. Vol. 1: Theoretical Studies towards a Sociology of Language.* London: Routledge and Kegan Paul.

Bernstein, B. (1973). *Class, Codes and Control. Vol. 2: Applied Studies towards a Sociology of Language.* London: Routledge and Kegan Paul.

Bernstein, B., and Henderson, D. (1969). "Social Class Differences in the Relevance of Language to Socialization," *Sociology* 3, No. 1.

Blank, M., and Solomon, F. (1968). "A Tutorial Programme to Develop Abstract Thinking in Socially Disadvantaged Pre-School Children," *Child Development* 39: 379–89.

Brandis, W., and Henderson, D. (1970). "Social Class, Language and Communication." *Primary Socialisation, Language and Education,* Vol. 1. Edited by B. Bernstein. London: Routledge and Kegan Paul.

Britton, J. (1970). *Language and Learning.* London and Baltimore, Md.: Penguin.

Brown, R. (1958). *Words and Things.* New York: Free Press.

Brown, R., and Bellugi, U., eds. (1964). *The Acquisition of Language.* Child Development Monographs.

Brown, R.; Cazden, C. B.; and Bellugi, U. (1969). *The Child's Grammar from I to III.* Edited by J. P. Hill. Minnesota Symposium on Child Psychology. Minneapolis: University of Minnesota Press.

Bruner, J. (1972). *The Relevance of Education.* London: George Allen & Unwin.

Cadzen, Courtney B. (1972). *Child Language and Education.* New York: Holt, Rinehart and Winston.

Cadzen, Courtney B., ed. (1972). *Language in Early Childhood Education.* Washington, D.C.: National Association for the Education of Young Children.

Church, J. (1961). *Language and the Discovery of Reality.* New York: Random House.

Creber, J. W. P. (1972). *Lost for Words.* London and Baltimore, Md.: Penguin.

Dean, J. (1968). *Reading, Writing and Talking.* London: Black.

Deutsch, M. (1962). *The Institute for Developmental Studies Annual Report and Descriptive Statement.* New York: New York University Press.

Deutsch, M. (1965). "The Role of Social Class in Language Development and Cognition," *American Journal of Orthopsychiatry* 35: 78-88.

Gahagan, D., and Gahagan, J. (1971). *Talk Reform.* Beverly Hills, Calif.: Sage.

Gray, S., and Klaus, R. A. (1965). "An Experimental Pre-School Program for Culturally Deprived Children," *Child Development* 36: 887-98.

Hess, R. D.; Block, M.; Costello, J.; Knowles, R. T.; and Largay, D. (1967). "Parent Involvement in Early Education," *Day Care: Resources for Decisions.* Edited by E. H. Grotberg. Washington, D.C.: Office of Economic Opportunity.

Hess, R. D., and Shipman, V. (1965). "Early Experience and the Socialisation of Cognitive Modes in Children," *Child Development* 36: 86-99.

Labov, W. (1970). "The Logic of Non-standard English." *Language and Poverty: Perspectives on a Theme.* Edited by F. Williams. Chicago: Markham, pp. 153–89.

Lawton, D. (1968). *Social Class, Language and Education.* London: Routledge and Kegan Paul.

Lewis, M. M. (1963). *Language, Thought and Personality in Infancy and Childhood.* London: Harrap.

Loban, W. D. (1963). *The Language of Elementary School Children.* Champaign, Ill.: National Council of Teachers of English (Research Report No. 1), Dunn, Horton, and Smith, 1968.

Luria, A. R., and Yudovich, F. J. (1972). *Speech and the Development of Mental Processes in the Child.* Baltimore, Md.: Penguin.

Peabody Language Development Kit, Level P. Circle Pines, Minn.: American Guidance Service.

Phillips, J. R. (1970). "Formal Characteristics of Speech Which Mothers Address to Their Young Children." Unpublished doctoral dissertation. Baltimore, Md.: Johns Hopkins University. Reported in C. B. Cazden (1972).

Piaget, J. (1955). *Language and Thought of the Child.* New York: Humanities, 3rd ed., 1962; New York: World Publishing, paperback ed., 1955.

Piaget, J., and Inhelder, B. (1969). *The Psychology of the Child.* New York: Basic Books.

Robinson, W. P., and Rackstraw, S. J. (1967). "Social and Psychological Factors Related to Variability of Answering Behavior in Five-Year-Old Children," *Language and Speech* 10, No. 2, 88.

Silverman, C., and Weikart, D. P. (in preparation). "Open Framework: Evaluation of a Concept in Pre-School Education," *National Elementary Principal.*

Snow, C. E. (1971). "Language Acquisition and Mothers' Speech to Children." Unpublished doctoral dissertation. Montreal, Canada: McGill University. Reported in C. B. Cazden (1972).

134 /

Strickland, R. (1962). "The Language of Elementary School Children," *Bulletin of the School of Education, Indiana University,* No. 38, p. 4.

Tough, Joan (in preparation). *The Development of Meaning. Vol. 1. A Study of Children's Use of Language.*

Tough, Joan, and Sestini, Elizabeth (in preparation). *The Development of Meaning. Vol. 2. A Study of the Language of Mothers and Their Children.*

Weikart, D. P., *et al.* (1971). *The Cognitively Oriented Curriculum: A Framework for Pre-School Teachers.* Washington, D.C.: National Association for the Education of Young Children.

Whorf, B. L. (1955). *Language, Thought and Reality.* Edited by J. B. Carroll. Cambridge, Mass.: M.I.T. Press.

Wilkinson, A. (1971). *The Foundations of Language.* New York: Oxford University Press.

Vygotsky, L. S. (1962). *Thought and Language.* Cambridge, Mass.: M.I.T. Press.

Index